Self-harm and Suicide

Series Editor: Cara Acred

Volume 258

Independence Educational Publishers

First published by Independence Educational Publishers

The Studio, High Green

Great Shelford

Cambridge CB22 5EG

England

© Independence 2014

Photocopy licence

The material in this book is protected by copyright. However, the

purchaser is free to make multiple copies of particular articles for instructional

purposes for immediate use within the purchasing institution.

Making copies of the entire book is not permitted.

British Library Cataloguing in Publication Data

Self-harm and suicide. -- (Issues ; 258)

1. Suicidal behavior--Great Britain.

2. Suicide--Great Britain.

3. Parasuicide--Great Britain.

4. Cutting (Self-mutilation)--Great Britain.

I. Series II. Acred, Cara editor of compilation.

362.2'8'0941-dc23

Self – harm and suicide

Pri   ain

Y362.
28

1944541

Contents

Chapter 1: What is self-harm?

Chapter 2: Suicide

Introduction

Self-harm and Suicide is Volume 258 in the **ISSUES** series. The aim of the series is to offer current, diverse information about important issues in our world, from a UK perspective.

ABOUT SELF-HARM AND SUICIDE

An estimated one in 12 children/young people are said to self-harm and, although it is not directly related to suicide, research has shown that about three in every 100 people who self-harm over 15 years will eventually kill themselves. This book deals with self-harm and suicide as two separate topics, exploring the reasons why people self-harm and experience suicidal thoughts. It also looks at coping mechanisms and real-life experiences, and at the recent links between cyberbullying and suicide.

OUR SOURCES

Titles in the **ISSUES** series are designed to function as educational resource books, providing a balanced overview of a specific subject.

The information in our books is comprised of facts, articles and opinions from many different sources, including:

⇨ Newspaper reports and opinion pieces

⇨ Website fact sheets

⇨ Magazine and journal articles

⇨ Statistics and surveys

⇨ Government reports

⇨ Literature from special interest groups.

A NOTE ON CRITICAL EVALUATION

Because the information reprinted here is from a number of different sources, readers should bear in mind the origin of the text and whether the source is likely to have a particular bias when presenting information (or when conducting their research). It is hoped that, as you read about the many aspects of the issues explored in this book, you will critically evaluate the information presented.

It is important that you decide whether you are being presented with facts or opinions. Does the writer give a biased or unbiased report? If an opinion is being expressed, do you agree with the writer? Is there potential bias to the 'facts' or statistics behind an article?

ASSIGNMENTS

In the back of this book, you will find a selection of assignments designed to help you engage with the articles you have been reading and to explore your own opinions. Some tasks will take longer than others and there is a mixture of design, writing and research-based activities that you can complete alone or in a group.

FURTHER RESEARCH

At the end of each article we have listed its source and a website that you can visit if you would like to conduct your own research. Please remember to critically evaluate any sources that you consult and consider whether the information you are viewing is accurate and unbiased.

Useful weblinks

www.helpguide.org

www.jasonfoundation.com

www.mentalhealth.org.uk

www.mind.org.uk

www.mindfull.org

www.nhs.uk

www.rcpsych.ac.uk

www.studentsagainstdepression.org

www.talkingtaboos.com

www.teenissues.co.uk

www.time-to-change.org.uk

www.youngminds.org.uk

Reporting suicide and self-harm

If you are tasked with reporting about suicide or self-harm it is really important to do this responsibly as studies have shown that some reporting can lead to copycat behaviour.

⇨ Focus on feelings, not behaviours. Try to report underlying issues or motivations behind the self-harm, as opposed to detailing the behaviour itself. Graphic descriptions can be used as tips by people who may be predisposed to self-harming.

⇨ Don't be explicit about methods, e.g. it may be okay to mention taking an overdose, but avoid detailing what substance was taken, how many tablets, etc. This could be used as a tip by someone experiencing suicidal ideations.

⇨ Avoid coverage of self-harming behaviours by celebrities. It could glamourise or prompt imitation behaviour.

⇨ Remember the correct term is to 'complete' suicide, not 'commit'. 'Commit' is used when describing criminality, and implies judgement or persecution.

⇨ Avoid phrases like 'unsuccessful suicide attempt'. This attributes feelings of achievement or failure to taking one's own life.

⇨ No images relating to self-injury should be used. This can be triggering and distressing for readers.

⇨ Avoid presenting the behaviour as an appropriate solution to the problems, as readers may interpret the behaviour as a positive coping strategy.

⇨ Avoid disclosing the contents of any suicide notes, past or present. Sometimes this may be used as guidance for a vulnerable person to justify their own suicide.

⇨ The above information is reprinted with kind permission from Time to Change. Please visit www.time-to-change.org.uk for further information.

© 2008 Time to Change

Self-harm

This article is for anyone who wants to know more about self-harm, particularly anyone who is harming themselves, or feels that they might. We hope it will also be helpful for friends and families.

The article looks at the different sorts of self-harm and why someone might do it. It discusses:

⇨ some of the help available

⇨ what you can do to help yourself

⇨ what friends or family can do to help.

What is self-harm?

Self-harm happens when you hurt or harm yourself. You may:

⇨ take too many tablets – an overdose

⇨ cut yourself

⇨ burn yourself

⇨ bang your head or throw yourself against something hard

⇨ punch yourself

⇨ stick things in your body

⇨ swallow things.

It can feel to other people that these things are done calmly and deliberately – almost cynically. But we know that someone who self-harms is usually in a state of high emotion, distress and unbearable inner turmoil. Some people plan it in advance; for others, it happens on the spur of the moment. Some people self-harm only once or twice, but others do it regularly – it can be hard to stop.

Some of us harm ourselves in less obvious, but still serious, ways. We may behave in ways that suggest we don't care whether we live or die – we may take drugs recklessly, have unsafe sex or binge drink. Some people simply starve themselves.

Other words that are used to describe self-harm

These terms were previously used to describe self-harm, but are now going out of use:

⇨ Deliberate self-harm (DSH): the word 'deliberate' tended to blame people for their self-harm.

⇨ Suicide/Parasuicide: these suggested that harming yourself is the same as wanting to kill yourself – which is often not the case.

How common is self-harm?

About one in ten young people will self-harm at some point, but it can happen at any age.

The research probably under-estimates how common self-harm is. It is usually based on surveys of people who go to hospital or their GP after harming themselves. However, we know that a lot of people do not seek help after self-harm. Some types of self-harm, like cutting, may be more secret and so less likely to be noticed.

In a recent study of over 4,000 self-harming adults in hospital, 80% had overdosed and around 15% had cut themselves. In the community, it is likely that cutting is a more common way of self-harming than taking an overdose.

Who self-harms?

It happens more often in:

⇨ young women

⇨ prisoners, asylum seekers and veterans of the armed forces

⇨ gay, lesbian and bisexual people: this seems, at least in part, due to the stress of prejudice and discrimination

⇨ a group of young people who self-harm together: having a friend who self-harms may increase your chances of doing it as well

⇨ people who have experienced physical, emotional or sexual abuse during childhood.

What makes people self-harm?

Research has shown that many people who harm themselves are struggling with intolerable distress or

YOU NEED HELP?

...HOW DID YOU KNOW?

unbearable situations. A person will often struggle with difficulties for some time before they self-harm.

Common problems include:

⇨ physical or sexual abuse

⇨ feeling depressed

⇨ feeling bad about yourself

⇨ relationship problems with partners, friends and family

⇨ being unemployed, or having difficulties at work.

You may be more likely to harm yourself if you feel:

⇨ that people don't listen to you

⇨ hopeless

⇨ isolated, alone

⇨ out of control

⇨ powerless – it feels as though there's nothing you can do to change anything.

It's more likely to happen if you are using alcohol or drugs – it may feel that these are as out of control as the rest of your life.

You may feel like harming yourself if you want to show someone else how distressed you are or to get back at them or to punish them. This is not common – most people suffer in silence and self-harm in private.

How does it make you feel?

Self-harm can help you to feel in control, and reduce uncomfortable feelings of tension and distress. If you feel guilty, it can be a way of punishing yourself and relieving your guilt. Either way, it can become a 'quick fix' for feeling bad.

Does this mean I'm mentally ill?

Probably not. However, you may be depressed, have personality difficulties, find it difficult to get on with other people or have problems with alcohol and/or drugs. You could still do with some help.

Is self-harm the same as attempted suicide?

Usually not. But if you start to harm yourself, the risk of killing yourself is greater than for people who don't self-harm. So anyone who self-harms should be taken seriously and offered help.

Getting help

A lot of people who self-harm don't ask for help. Why not? You might be aware that you have some serious problems, but don't feel that you can tell anyone – so you don't talk about it. You may not feel that you do have a serious problem, but see self-harm as a way to cope with life. Unfortunately, at the moment, if you do go to hospital after self-harming, you've only got a 50:50 chance of being seen by a specialist in this area.

Danger signs

You are most likely to harm yourself badly if you:

⇨ use a dangerous or violent method

⇨ self-harm regularly

⇨ don't see many people

⇨ have a mental illness.

You should really see someone who has a lot of experience of helping people who self-harm, and who knows about mental health problems.

What help is there?

Talking with a non-professional

You may find it helpful just to talk anonymously to someone else about what is happening to you. Knowing that someone else knows what you are going through can help you to feel less alone with your problems. It can also help you to think about your difficulties more clearly – maybe even see ways of solving them that you wouldn't think of on your own. You can do this on the Internet or by telephone. Telephone helplines are listed at the end of this article.

Self-help groups

A group of people, who all self-harm, meet regularly to give each other emotional support and practical advice. Just sharing your problems in a group can help you to feel less alone – others in the group will almost certainly have had similar experiences.

Help with relationships

Self-harm is often the result of a crisis in a close relationship. If this is the case, get some help with sorting out the relationship – it may be more difficult in the short-term, but it will be better for you (certainly less dangerous) in the long-term.

Talking with a professional

One-to-one talking treatments can help, such as:

⇨ Problem-solving therapy

⇨ Cognitive behavioural therapy

⇨ Psychodynamic psychotherapy

⇨ Family meetings.

If you are still living with your family, it may help to have a family meeting with a therapist. This can help to relieve the tiring, daily stress for everyone in the family. It is not always appropriate, for instance, if you are the victim of physical or sexual abuse within your family.

Group therapy

This is different from a self-help group. A professional will lead (or facilitate) the group to help the members to deal with problems they share; for example, in getting on with other people.

What works best?

There isn't much good evidence yet of which therapies work well for people who have harmed themselves. However, what evidence there is, suggests that problem-solving therapy and cognitive-behavioural therapy are useful. A health professional will make suggestions based on your individual problems and on what is available locally.

What if I don't get help?

About one in three people who self-harm for the first time will do it again during the following year.

About one in 100 people who self-harm over 15 years will actually kill themselves. This is more than 50 times the rate for people who don't self-harm. The risk increases with age and is much greater for men.

Cutting can give you permanent scarring. If nerves or tendons are damaged by cutting, this can lead to numbness or weakness.

How can I help myself?

The feelings of self-harm will go away after a while. If you can cope with your distress without self-harming for a time, it will get easier over the next few hours. You can:

⇨ Talk to someone – if you are on your own perhaps you could phone a friend. Telephone helplines are listed at the end of this article.

⇨ If the person you are with is making you feel worse, go out.

⇨ Distract yourself by going out, listening to music or by doing something harmless that interests you.

⇨ Relax and focus your mind on something pleasant – your very own personal comforting place.

⇨ Find another way to express your feelings such as squeezing ice cubes (which you can make with red juice to mimic blood if the sight of blood is important), or just drawing red lines on your skin.

⇨ Give yourself some 'harmless pain' – eat a hot chilli, or have a cold shower.

⇨ Focus your mind on positive things.

⇨ Be kind to yourself – allow yourself to do something harmless that you enjoy.

⇨ Write a diary or a letter, to explain what is happening to you – no one else needs to see it.

When you don't feel like harming yourself

When the urge has gone, and you feel safe, think about the times that you have self-harmed and what (if anything) has been helpful.

⇨ Go back in your mind to the last time when you did not want to self-harm, and move forward in your memory from there.

⇨ Think about where you were, who you were with and what you were feeling?

⇨ Try to work out why you began feeling like you did.

⇨ Did your self-harm give you a sense of escape, or relief

or control? Try to work out something to do that might give you the same result, but that doesn't damage you.

⇨ How did other people react?

⇨ Could you have done anything else?

⇨ Make an audio recording. Talk about your good points and why you don't want to self-harm. Or, ask someone you trust to do this. When you start to feel bad, you can play this back to remind yourself of the parts of you that are good and worthwhile.

⇨ Make a 'crisis plan' so you can talk to someone instead of self-harming. Being able to get in touch with someone quickly can help you control your urge to self-harm. While you are talking, your wish to harm yourself may start to go away.

What if you don't want to stop self-harming?

If you decide that you don't want to stop self-harming, you can still:

⇨ reduce the damage to your body (for example, by using clean blades if you cut yourself)

⇨ keep thinking about possible answers to the things that make you harm yourself

⇨ every so often, re-consider your decision not to stop.

Self-harm can be very damaging physically and psychologically – in the end, you'll do better by stopping.

There are a number of questions to ask yourself to see if you are ready to stop. If you can honestly say YES to half of the questions below, or more, then why not try stopping?

⇨ Are there at least two people who are willing to help me stop?

⇨ Do I have friends that know about my self-harming who I can go to if I get desperate?

⇨ Have I found at least two alternative safe ways that reduce the feelings that lead me to self-harm?

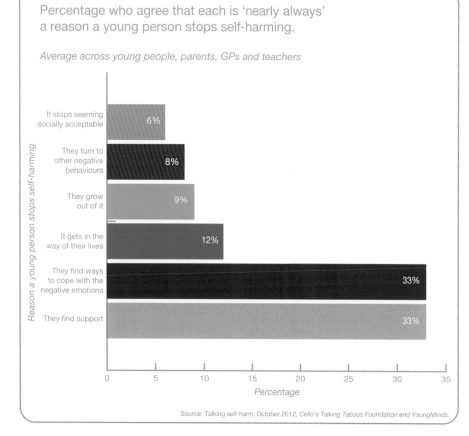

Percentage who agree that each is 'nearly always' a reason a young person stops self-harming.

Average across young people, parents, GPs and teachers

Reason a young person stops self-harming

- It stops seeming socially acceptable — 6%
- They turn to other negative behaviours — 8%
- They grow out of it — 9%
- It gets in the way of their lives — 12%
- They find ways to cope with the negative emotions — 33%
- They find support — 33%

Percentage (0, 5, 10, 15, 20, 25, 30, 35)

Source: Talking self-harm, October 2012, Cello's Talking Taboos Foundation and YoungMinds.

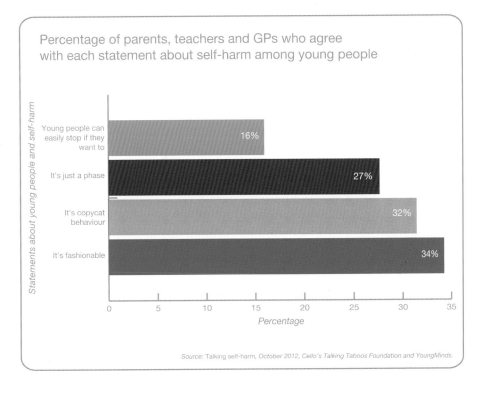

Percentage of parents, teachers and GPs who agree with each statement about self-harm among young people

Statements about young people and self-harm

Young people can easily stop if they want to	16%
It's just a phase	27%
It's copycat behaviour	32%
It's fashionable	34%

Percentage

Source: *Talking self-harm*, October 2012, Cello's Talking Taboos Foundation and YoungMinds.

⇨ Am I able to tell myself, and to believe, that I want to stop hurting myself?

⇨ Can I tell myself that I WILL tolerate feelings of frustration, desperation and fear?

⇨ If necessary, is there a professional who will also give me support and help in a crisis?

If I harm myself and need treatment?

You have the right to be treated with courtesy and respect by the doctors and nurses in the Emergency Department.

Many Emergency Departments now have easy access to a health professional who knows about self-harm, such as a psychiatric nurse or doctor or a social worker. They will be able to talk with you about how you are feeling and to see if there are any ways of helping you. They should be able to properly assess all your needs, whatever they may be. You should be able to go through your assessment with them. Staff may want to go through a questionnaire with you, to try to judge how at risk you are.

What can I do if I know someone who self-harms?

It can be very upsetting to be close to someone who self-harms – but there are things you can do. The most important is to listen to them without judging them or being critical. This can be very hard if you are upset yourself – and perhaps angry – about what they are doing. Try to concentrate on them rather than your own feelings – although this can be hard.

Do

⇨ Talk to them when they feel like self-harming. Try to understand their feelings, and then move the conversation onto other things.

⇨ Take some of the mystery out of self-harm by helping them find out about self-harm perhaps by showing them this article, or by using the Internet or the local library.

⇨ Find out about getting help – maybe go with them to see someone, such as their GP.

⇨ Help them to think about their self-harm not as a shameful secret, but as a problem to be sorted out.

Don't

⇨ Try to be their therapist – therapy is complicated and you have enough to deal with as their friend, partner or relative.

⇨ Expect them to stop overnight – it's difficult and takes time and effort.

⇨ React strongly, with anger, hurt or upset – this is likely to make them feel worse. Talk honestly about the effect it has on you, but do this calmly and in a way that shows how much you care for them.

⇨ Struggle with them when they are about to self-harm – it's better to walk away and to suggest they come and talk about it rather than do it.

⇨ Make them promise not to do it again.

⇨ Say that you won't see them unless they stop self-harming.

⇨ Feel responsible for their self-harm or become the person who is supposed to stop them. You must get on with your own life as well. Make sure you talk to someone close to you, so you get some support.

Self-help and support

ChildLine

Free national helpline for young people, free confidential advice on all sorts of problems: 0800 1111.

Samaritans

Telephone and e-mail support for anyone who is worried, upset or suicidal; 08457 90 90 90; ROI 1850 60 90 90; e-mail: jo@samaritans.org.

NHS Direct

A helpline with health advice – now call either 0845 4647 (depending on your area) or 111.

Updated January 2012

⇨ The above information is reprinted with kind permission from the Royal College of Psychiatrists. Please visit www.rcpsych.ac.uk for further information.

© 2013 Royal College of Psychiatrists

Self-harm and cutting

Self-injury help, support and treatment.

Self-harm can be a way of coping with problems. It may help you express feelings you can't put into words, distract you from your life or release emotional pain. Afterwards, you probably feel better – at least for a little while. But then the painful feelings return and you feel the urge to hurt yourself again. If you want to stop but don't know how, remember this: you deserve to feel better and you can get there without hurting yourself.

Understanding cutting and self-harm

Self-harm is a way of expressing and dealing with deep distress and emotional pain. As counterintuitive as it may sound to those on the outside, hurting yourself makes you feel better. In fact, you may feel like you have no choice. Injuring yourself is the only way you know how to cope with feelings like sadness, self-loathing, emptiness, guilt and rage.

The problem is that the relief that comes from self-harming doesn't last very long. It's like slapping on a plaster when what you really need are stitches. It may temporarily stop the bleeding, but it doesn't fix the underlying injury. And it also creates its own problems.

If you're like most people who self-injure, you try to keep what you're doing secret. Maybe you feel ashamed or maybe you just think that no one would understand. But hiding who you are and what you feel is a heavy burden. Ultimately, the secrecy and guilt affects your relationships with your friends and family members and the way you feel about yourself. It can make you feel even more lonely, worthless and trapped.

Myths and facts about cutting and self-harm

Because cutting and other means of self-harm tend to be taboo

subjects, the people around you – and possibly even you – may harbour serious misconceptions about your motivations and state of mind. Don't let these myths get in the way of getting help or helping someone you care about.

Myth: People who cut and self-injure are trying to get attention

Fact: The painful truth is that people who self-harm generally do so in secret. They aren't trying to manipulate others or draw attention to themselves. In fact, shame and fear can make it very difficult to come forward and ask for help.

Myth: People who self-injure are crazy and/or dangerous

Fact: It is true that many people who self-harm suffer from anxiety, depression or a previous trauma – just like millions of others in the general population. Self-injury is how they cope. Slapping them with

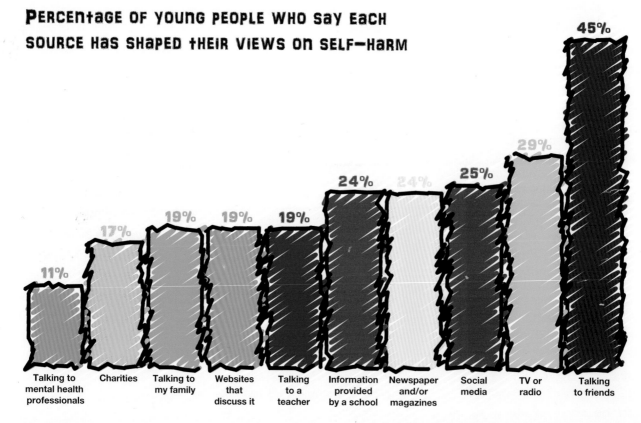

PERCENTAGE OF YOUNG PEOPLE WHO SAY EACH SOURCE HAS SHAPED THEIR VIEWS ON SELF-HARM

- Talking to mental health professionals — 11%
- Charities — 17%
- Talking to my family — 19%
- Websites that discuss it — 19%
- Talking to a teacher — 19%
- Information provided by a school — 24%
- Newspaper and/or magazines — 24%
- Social media — 25%
- TV or radio — 29%
- Talking to friends — 45%

Source: Talking self-harm, October 2012, Cello's Talking Taboos Foundation and YoungMinds.

a 'crazy' or 'dangerous' label isn't accurate or helpful.

Myth: People who self-injure want to die

Fact: Self-injurers usually do not want to die. When they self-harm, they are not trying to kill themselves – they are trying to cope with their pain. In fact, self-injury may be a way of helping themselves go on living. However, in the long-term, people who self-injure have a much higher risk of suicide, which is why it's so important to seek help.

Myth: If the wounds aren't bad, it's not that serious

Fact: The severity of a person's wounds has very little to do with how much he or she may be suffering. Don't assume that because the wounds or injuries are minor, there's nothing to worry about.

Signs and symptoms of cutting and self-harm

Self-harm includes anything you do to intentionally injure yourself. Some of the more common ways include:

⇨ cutting or severely scratching your skin

⇨ burning or scalding yourself

⇨ hitting yourself or banging your head

⇨ punching things or throwing your body against walls and hard objects

⇨ sticking objects into your skin

⇨ intentionally preventing wounds from healing

⇨ swallowing poisonous substances or inappropriate objects.

Self-harm can also include less obvious ways of hurting yourself or putting yourself in danger, such as driving recklessly, binge drinking, taking too many drugs and having unsafe sex.

Warning signs that a family member or friend is cutting or self-injuring

Because clothing can hide physical injuries, and inner turmoil can be covered up by a seemingly calm disposition, self-injury can be hard to detect. However, there are red flags you can look for (but remember – you don't have to be sure that you know what's going on in order to reach out to someone you're worried about):

⇨ Unexplained wounds or scars from cuts, bruises or burns, usually on the wrists, arms, thighs or chest.

⇨ Blood stains on clothing, towels or bedding; blood-soaked tissues.

⇨ Sharp objects or cutting instruments, such as razors, knives, needles, glass shards or bottle caps, in the person's belongings.

⇨ Frequent 'accidents'. Someone who self-harms may claim to be clumsy or have many mishaps, in order to explain away injuries.

⇨ Covering up. A person who self-injures may insist on wearing long sleeves or long pants, even in hot weather.

⇨ Needing to be alone for long periods of time, especially in the bedroom or bathroom.

⇨ Isolation and irritability.

How does cutting and self-harm help?

It's important to acknowledge that self-harm helps you – otherwise you wouldn't do it. Some of the ways cutting and self-harming can help include:

⇨ Expressing feelings you can't put into words

⇨ Releasing the pain and tension you feel inside

⇨ Helping you feel in control

⇨ Distracting you from overwhelming emotions or difficult life circumstances

⇨ Relieving guilt and punishing yourself

⇨ Making you feel alive, or simply feel something, instead of feeling numb.

Once you better understand why you self-harm, you can learn ways to stop self-harming and find resources that can support you through this struggle.

If self-harm helps, why stop?

Although self-harm and cutting can give you temporary relief, it comes at a cost. In the long term, it causes far more problems than it solves.

The relief is short lived, and is quickly followed by other feelings like shame and guilt. Meanwhile, it keeps you from learning more effective strategies for feeling better.

Keeping the secret from friends and family members is difficult and lonely.

You can hurt yourself badly, even if you don't mean to. It's easy to misjudge the depth of a cut or end up with an infected wound.

If you don't learn other ways to deal with emotional pain, it puts you at risk for bigger problems down the line, including major depression, drug and alcohol addiction and suicide.

Self-harm can become addictive. It may start off as an impulse or something you do to feel more in control, but soon it feels like the cutting or self-harming is controlling you. It often turns into a compulsive behaviour that seems impossible to stop.

The bottom line: self-harm and cutting don't help you with the issues that made you want to hurt yourself in the first place.

⇨ The above information is reprinted with kind permission from Helpguide. Please visit www.helpguide.org for further information.

The truth about self-harm

By Rebecca Whitefoot

Self-harmers are attention-seeking, manipulative teenagers. Self-harmers are suicidal. Self-harmers are goths. Self-harmers can stop if they want to. Self-harm is when you cut yourself with a knife. Myth. Myth. Myth. Myth. Myth!

How have we ended up getting it so wrong when it comes to sorting out self-harm fact from fiction?

Self-harm has a stigma that just won't budge. This is largely due to a lack of education and information available in schools and the NHS. In the Samaritans report *Youth Matters – A Cry For Help* 43% of young people knew someone who has self-harmed, but one-in-four didn't know what to say to a friend who was self-harming.

We have the highest level of self-harm in Europe. Around 25,000 11- to 25-year-olds are admitted to Accident and Emergency each year in England because of self-harming. Of course this number is nowhere near the actual amount of people who harm themselves, because many people will administer first-aid at home and never seek help.

Statistics show a worrying imbalance. An estimated one in 12 young adults has cut themselves, a massive percentage, and yet education on prevention, support and recovery of self-harm just isn't there. In the same report by the Samaritans, 41% of young people believed that self-harm was selfish and 55% of people thought it was stupid. It's time we got informed about an issue, which can wreak havoc on an individual's life, influencing everything from what they wear, to the relationships they have. We need to ask ourselves why there is such a large problem in the UK.

The motivations and methods used differ from one person to the next. Self-harm can be defined as burning, scalding, stabbing, banging heads and other body parts against walls, hair pulling, biting, breaking bones, jumping from heights or in front of vehicles, and swallowing or inserting objects.

Self-harmers may also overdose with medicine(s) or poisonous substances. This is called self-poisoning.

There is no 'type' of person that self-harms. The onset can start at seven-years-old or at 50-years-old. And there is no definitive reason why a person begins. One reason may be that the individual feels issues in their life are out of control.

The act of self-harming can give that person a sense of control. They may be suffering with feelings of loneliness, isolation, stress and frustration. They may be battling with low self-esteem and poor body image. Work pressures, money worries, and cultural and racial difficulties can all contribute. As do relationship problems, drug and alcohol issues, family breakdowns, bullying or bereavement.

One misconception, that needs to be dissolved, is that people who self-harm are trying to kill themselves. This is rarely the case as Frances McCann, a senior mental health practitioner explains, 'There's a big difference between someone saying they self-harm when they feel angry and a young person saying that they can't go on any more and want to end everything.'

The truth is the intention to commit suicide is only present in 15% of people. Self-harmers may harm to release and regulate their emotions. When the pressures of life become too high, self-harm becomes a safety valve – a way of relieving built-up tension. In an inquiry into self-harm published in the *Truth Hurts* report, 'a national inquiry into self-harm among young people', one respondent said, 'I don't deal with daily stress well, so when extra events occur, however big or small, my tension levels rise, resulting in my needing "release". Self-harm has proven to be most successful in this.'

The report found that after self-harming the person might feel calmer and more focused.

'It sounds awful but I felt I was a nicer person when I cut... balanced, normal.'

Self-harm can be an act of punishment in response to deep-rooted feelings of guilt and shame.

The pain of a cut can temporarily divert the individual's attention away from inner mental turmoil. Sometimes it can feel like the blood is taking away all the bad feelings.

Some people said that self-harming made them feel reconnected with reality, 'Sometimes when I felt numb and empty, scratching myself helped me to feel emotions again. It brought me back to life again.'

Self-harmers can go to great lengths to conceal their wounds, such as wearing long-sleeved tops or tights in sweltering conditions. However, if the wounds are on show some people see this as 'attention seeking'. This is yet another myth that must be banished.

Self-harmers find it immensely challenging to talk about their feelings of unhappiness and so they show their wounds as they feel this is the only way of communicating to other people how they're feeling inside and that they need help. As one self-harmer said, 'If someone's crying for help, don't stand there and judge the way in which they are asking for it.'

The inquiry also found that young people have been met with ridicule and hostility when they turned to professionals for help and that GPs are not sure how to approach the issue directly. Many self-harmers have had negative experiences when attending A & E.

'A & E isn't usually a positive experience. The last time I had a blood transfusion the consultant said I was wasting blood. The consultants there act as if to say, "Not you again".'

Many self-harmers will hide their activities from their family and friends because they are worried about the potential emotional impact. They fear their friends will view them differently once they've discussed their problems and in some instances, this becomes a reality.

Why are we, as a society, so worried about 'burdening' people with our problems? Why don't we talk more?

A self-harmer can feel guilt, shame and embarrassment about what they do to themselves. But why should self-harmers feel what they do is shameful or dirty when we accept eating disorders, alcoholism and drug abuse as serious mental conditions that require professional support and guidance?

I spoke to a group of students at Winchester University about why they think the UK has such a high level of self-harm and why it still holds such a negative stigma.

One student said, 'I avoid discussing self-harm because I am afraid that I could be talking to someone who is in fact a self-harmer. It's the act of inflicting injury on yourself that is still so taboo.'

She went on to explain that self-harm was so prevalent in our society but shrouded in secrecy. She said that this meant that a friend might be a self-harmer or have self-harmed and she wouldn't know. She said that, 'Alcoholism is more accepted than self-harm.' And that there are services such as Talk To Frank from which you can educate yourself about drugs, but there is no such service for self-harm.

Because of this lack of information those who disclose their problem to family and friends are often met with silence. The family and friends don't know how to respond since they are not educated on the subject.

Another student said that the 'go go go' work culture and fast-paced lifestyle in England makes people stressed and tense. Self-harm becomes an outlet for this tension. We need to slow down and ease off the pressures, they suggested.

Another student said we have adopted an 'American culture' in which everyone must be perfect and beautiful. Self-harm is an ugly blotch on this ideology and is therefore met with disapproval and disgust. She said we have put too high an expectation on ourselves and so when we can't cope with life it's like we have failed.

She added that films have a lot to answer for self-harm stereotypes. They do not portray self-harm in a realistic way, and often characters who self-harm will be 'goths' or 'stunningly beautiful teenagers' that glamourise the subject.

Thankfully steps are being made to get self-harm out there. A website, thesite.org, has recently launched a self-harm advice section, which is a fantastic resource for anyone affected.

The resource has been created by 42nd Street, Depaul UK and Youthnet (the charity that runs thesite.org), in response to the National Inquiry into self-harm.

Vera Martin, Director of 42nd Street, said, 'Self-harm is often misunderstood and frequently caricatured as attention seeking on the part of the young people who do it. But for many people self-harm is a response to – even a way of managing – deep-seated emotional distress and pain.'

For some people self-harm becomes an addictive cycle, a method of coping with the realities of our stressful, unpredictable lives. Breaking the cycle is tough, as the self-harmer will have to learn to go through the motions of hurt, anger, stress and grief without using that coping method. Self-harmers need the support and understanding of those around them.

We all have our own coping mechanisms. Some of us smoke, some of us drink alcohol, some of us exercise and some of us grab another bar of chocolate. Judging one person's coping method compared to another does not help. Getting to the bottom of why we need a coping mechanism in the first place is the key.

You can discover this by chatting to family, friends, going onto thesite.org discussion board or going to see a counsellor.

Talking about self-harm and informing yourself about it is the direction we all need to take to change the status of this stigma against self-harmers.

⇨ The above information is reprinted with kind permission from The National Student. Please visit www.thenationalstudent.com for further information.

Talking self-harm

An extract from the report by YoungMinds and Cello's Talking Taboos Foundation.

At YoungMinds we deal with self-harm a lot. The ways we do it vary but they include: our Parents' Helpline; our training courses for teachers; youth workers and service providers; our lobbying work with government officials and our work directly with young people.

Mental health problems don't just affect particular groups; they span all races, cultures and classes, and self-harm is no exception. Self-harm is surrounded by myths and misconceptions – while it's often just thought of in terms of cutting, self-harm or self-injury, describes a wide range of things people deliberately do to themselves that are harmful but usually do not kill them. It's worth noting that while self-harm is usually not an attempt at suicide, it is still highly traumatic for young people and those who care for them.

The symptoms

The most common form of self-harm is cutting the arms or the back of the legs with a razor or knife, but it takes many forms, including burning, biting, hitting and taking overdoses.

The reasons vary greatly, and are specific to the individual, but a young person may self-harm to help them cope with negative feelings, to feel more in control or to punish themselves. It can be a way of relieving overwhelming feelings that build up inside, when they feel isolated, angry, guilty or desperate.

The stats

One in 12 children and young people are said to self-harm and over the last ten years inpatient admissions for young people who self-harm have increased by 68%. In the last year alone these hospital admissions for under-25s increased by 10%. And, among females under 25, there has been a 77% increase in the last ten years.

Causes

Worryingly, as the hospital figures are only the tip of the iceberg, the true figure of how many children and young people are self-harming is likely to be far higher, and this is especially so for particular at-risk groups including lesbian and gay, transgender and bisexual young people, looked-after children, and young people in the criminal justice system.

Self-harm is surrounded in guilt, shame and mystery for all parties. Parents often confide in us that they feel it's their fault their child is harming themselves; teachers tell us they see the signs but cannot bring themselves to say anything, and even if they want to, they can't find the words to reach out to young people; and the children and young people we work with say over and over again, 'I need help, I am in terrible pain inside.'

And it's getting worse. More and more children and young people are using self-harm as a mechanism to cope with the pressures of life. Self-harm is often dismissed as merely attention-seeking behaviour but it's a sign that young people are feeling terrible internal pain and are not coping.

Young people today are growing up in a harsh environment with increasing stress to perform at school, low job prospects and the constant pressure to keep up with the latest consumer trends. And social networking, although creating ever greater circles of 'friends', often leaves young people feeling even more isolated and alone.

> **'A young person may self-harm to help them cope with negative feelings, to feel more in control or to punish themselves'**

Making progress

When we first met representatives from the Cello group we liked the idea of their Talking Taboos initiative and felt that if there was one thing that really was a taboo and needed talking about it was self-harm. Some cynicism was expressed about corporates just trying to make themselves look good by doing research on a controversial issue. However, our experience of working with the Cello group demonstrated that this couldn't be further from the truth. They have put their hearts and souls and over a quarter of a million pounds worth of their time into researching what parents, teachers, healthcare professionals and young people themselves know and feel about self-harm.

This is a ground-breaking piece of research about public attitudes, and its results highlight a comprehensive range of insights that we need to act on. If we don't we will not only continue to waste millions of pounds in treating entrenched mental illness when we could have intervened early, but we will keep failing the thousands of young people who are crying out for help, and the teachers, GPs and parents who really want to support them but don't know how to.

23 October 2012

⇨ The above information is reprinted with kind permission from YoungMinds and Cello's Talking Taboos Foundation. Please visit www.youngminds.org.uk, www.talkingtaboos.com or www.cellogroup.com/pdfs/talking_self_harm.pdf for further information.

The first time I said 'I self-harm'

Warning, some readers may find this post triggering.

Hi, my name is Suzi and I am a self-harmer but I am seven and a half years cut free. That's how I think of self-harming. I don't self-harm now but I am always in recovery, just like being in AA.

I started self-harming from a young age but it was at university that things unravelled for me. I found more and more that I was on a self-destructive path and the self-harming got worse. I seemed to start suffering from depression, I stopped going to lectures, I was smoking cannabis a lot, I was drinking a lot, I wasn't sleeping and my hair started to fall out.

My sister, who went to the same university, knew something wasn't right and did show concern but she didn't know the true extent of what was going on. I was in my second year of a law degree and there was no way I was going to pass the second year. My housemates noticed I was self-harming more and one of them tried to reach out to me. She sent me a beautiful card listing ten reasons why she loved me – it was hard to read. She finished the card by asking me not to hurt myself and added because it hurts her, to see me hurting. She never said it to my face or asked me, no one did.

The first time I said the words 'I self-harm'

I was encouraged to go and see my mentor- who was a university lecturer – and although I didn't explain everything, he suggested I talk to the doctor at uni. So I did. She said to put my second year on hold, I had to tell her exactly what was going on and why I was self medicating with cannabis and alcohol. I didn't want to tell her but knew that she wouldn't be able to sign me off without giving her something. So the first time I said the words 'I self-harm' was to a random doctor. I wasn't enjoying my course and I wonder if I was ever destined to finish my law degree. But, I definitely was not in the best place to get the results I was capable of.

I was signed off for a year and was told I had to go for counselling to address the issues that were causing me to self-harm. I didn't go back to uni. I got a couple of jobs to keep me going and pay my rent. So I worked but I continued to drink too much and smoke cannabis and then I met someone. Who knew that nine years on we would be married! Things changed.

My boyfriend wasn't horrified or ashamed of me

Into the first year of our relationship, my then boyfriend, now husband, asked me what my scars were and why I did it. I didn't have an answer then but I did tell him what I did to myself. All of it. I laid it all bare for him to see my emotional nakedness. And he didn't go anywhere. So the first person I really confided in (the doctor didn't count), didn't run a mile. In fact, he wasn't horrified or ashamed of me. He was sad. He was sad that I felt I had to do it. He asked me to never do it again and to talk to him. And to be honest, I had a few slips in that first year or two, as I had nowhere to hide it from my boyfriend.

Taking the time to reflect on my life, I now understand why my family, who knew, didn't want to ask me why I did it and felt they couldn't ask me to stop: they were frightened of the answer. Or frightened that I would go off the rails and do it more. Or perhaps they were worried I would say it was because of them.

I can only now admit to myself why I did it

I know now that I self-harm to deal with my frustration and anger – usually at myself, and it started with my parents' divorce. Self-harming, for me, was a compulsion. I don't place any blame on anyone. Not even on myself. It was just my way of dealing with those feelings and it isn't until some 18 years later I can admit that to myself. I self-stigmatise. I can only now admit to myself why I did it, why I always think about doing it, but why I hopefully will never do it again.

I recently went through two miscarriages – the most emotional last six months of mine and my husband's lives. I didn't self-harm. I thought about it, as I always do, but never had any intention to do it. It was then that I realised I am strong enough to share my story.

All I needed was for someone to support me

I always thought it was my family and friends that showed stigma towards my 'situation' by not really talking about it and sweeping it under the carpet. By alluding to it and making reference to it, but never discussing 'it'. But it wasn't, it was me self-stigmatising. I now realise that it must be a really hard thing for a family member or a friend to see someone clearly struggling and doing so by hurting themselves, and perhaps worrying that that person might go off the rails. From my experience, I know all I needed was for someone to ask me, to support me, to love me and then give me time to reflect on the reasons why.

Hi, my name is Suzi and I am a self-harmer... I intend to be cut free forever.

10 January 2013

⇨ The above information is reprinted with kind permission from Time to Change. Please visit www.time-to-change.org.uk for further information.

Coping with self-harming urges

Deliberate self-harm is a behaviour distinct from attempting suicide. For some people it becomes a 'coping strategy' for dealing with overwhelming or painful feelings. Coping with the urges to self-harm requires learning different ways to deal with these feelings.

Read with caution

This information has been provided to allow you to think constructively about your self-harming behaviour. However, if you are aware that reading about self-harm practices might feel 'triggering' for you then make sure you read this with someone else present or find another way to reduce the risk.

Work on things step by step

If self-harming has become a kind of coping strategy, it is not usually helpful to focus on complete abstinence or banning the behaviour in one sudden step. Instead, it is helpful to build new strategies for dealing with difficult feelings which can gradually take the place of self-harm. In the first instance it can be useful to consider learning first aid and knowing how to take care of yourself practically if you do self-harm.

Creating a personal self-harm safety plan is a useful way to remind yourself of things you can do when you feel an urge to self-harm. These include ways to manage and reduce self-harming behaviours in the short term, so that they are less damaging, as well as alternative ways to manage difficult feelings which can replace self-harm in the longer term.

De-escalate the intensity of self-harm

A first step can be to think about trying to slowly reduce the damage caused by your self-harming behaviour (e.g. cutting less deeply). Then try to move to less damaging practices like writing on your skin with red felt tip instead of cutting.

Direct the harming urge at something else

Some people find squeezing an ice cube provides an alternative that is helpful. Hit pillows or cushions. Flick an elastic band on your wrist. Take a cold bath or shower.

Make a list of distractions

Make a list of activities that you can use to distract yourself. Trying to be with other people is particularly effective.

Know your triggers and reduce the risks

Knowing what kinds of situations are particularly risky for you can help you plan to reduce the risks. For example, it is harder to manage your feelings effectively when you are under the influence of drugs or alcohol. Go easy on these if you are aware that you are feeling less stable.

Learn to tune in to your feelings

In the longer term you can start to learn how to identify the experiences and feelings which are most likely to trigger your urges to self-harm. Learning the skill of 'mindfulness' – being tuned in to what you are feeling in the present moment, without judgement or attempt to change it – is invaluable in the move towards being able to manage or 'ride out' difficult feelings, rather than trying to eliminate them.

Find constructive outlets for feelings

Having a good cry is the natural way to get rid of built up stress hormones and get feelings out. Experiment with different ways to express feelings when they seem to be building up inside, to see what works for you. Keeping a diary can be a useful habit for getting feelings 'out'. Just write it all down without censorship, then close it and put it away. Or it might be helpful to do something symbolic like writing it all down then scribbling it out or tearing it up. Vigorous activity or exercise can be another helpful way to get rid of pent up feelings.

Learn how to self soothe

Make a conscious effort to take care of yourself and comfort yourself with difficult feelings. Try out different things to see what you find most comforting. Breathing and relaxation exercises can be very useful. A relaxing soak in a bubble bath, hugs or a massage, eating something sweet (in moderation), stroking a pet, listening to uplifting music, knitting or crafts... Find what works for you!

Get support and professional help

Having people you can talk to and a good support network is a vital protection against both self-harm and suicidal thinking.

Talking about the inner feelings that fuel your self-harm is potentially useful whoever you talk to, but counsellors are professionally trained to work with self-harm and will be best placed to support you in finding constructive alternatives.

⇨ The above material is from studentsagainstdepression. org, a project of the Charlie Waller Memorial Trust. Intellectual property rights for the site are owned by Dr Denise Meyer. We are grateful to the Trust for allowing us to use their material.

Help for cutting and self-harm

Step 1: Confide in someone

If you're ready to get help for cutting or self-harm, the first step is to confide in another person. It can be scary to talk about the very thing you have worked so hard to hide, but it can also be a huge relief to finally let go of your secret and share what you're going through.

Deciding whom you can trust with such personal information can be difficult. Choose someone who isn't going to gossip or try to take control of your recovery. Ask yourself who in your life makes you feel accepted and supported. It could be a friend, teacher, religious leader, counsellor or relative. But you don't necessarily have to choose someone you are close to.

Eventually, you'll want to open up to your inner circle of friends and family members, but sometimes it's easier to start by talking to an adult who you respect – such as a teacher, religious leader or counsellor – who has a little more distance from the situation and won't find it as difficult to be objective.

Tips for talking about cutting and self-harm

⇨ Focus on your feelings. Instead of sharing sensational details of your self-harm behaviour – what specifically you do to hurt yourself – focus on the feelings or situations that lead to it. This can help the person you're confiding in better understand where you're coming from. It also helps to let the person know why you're telling them. Do you want help or advice from them? Do you simply want another person to know so you can let go of the secret?

⇨ Communicate in whatever way you feel most comfortable. If you're too nervous to talk in person, consider starting off the conversation with an e-mail or letter (although it's important to eventually follow up with a face-to-face conversation). Don't feel pressured into sharing things you're not ready to talk about. You don't have to show the person your injuries or answer any questions you don't feel comfortable answering.

⇨ Give the person time to process what you tell them. As difficult as it is for you to open up, it may also be difficult for the person you tell – especially if it's a close friend or family member. Sometimes, you may not like the way the person reacts. Try to remember that reactions such as shock, anger and fear come out of concern for you. It may help to photocopy or print out this article for the people you choose to tell. The better they understand self-harm, the better able they'll be to support you.

Talking about self-harm can be very stressful and bring up a lot of emotions. Don't be discouraged if the situation feels worse for a short time right after sharing your secret. It's uncomfortable to confront and change long-standing habits. But once you get past these initial challenges, you'll start to feel better.

Step 2: Figure out why you cut

Learn to manage overwhelming stress and emotions

Understanding why you cut or self-harm is a vital first step towards your recovery. If you can figure out what function your self-injury serves, you can learn other ways to get those needs met – which in turn can reduce your desire to hurt yourself.

Identify your self-harm triggers

Remember, self-harm is most often a way of dealing with emotional pain. What feelings make you want to cut or hurt yourself? Sadness? Anger? Shame? Loneliness? Guilt? Emptiness?

Once you learn to recognise the feelings that trigger your need to self-injure, you can start developing healthier alternatives.

Get in touch with your feelings

If you're having a hard time pinpointing the feelings that trigger your urge to cut, you may need to work on your emotional awareness. Emotional awareness means knowing what you are feeling and why. It's the ability to identify and express what you are feeling from moment to moment and to understand the connection between your feelings and your actions.

The idea of paying attention to your feelings – rather than numbing them or releasing them through self-harm – may sound frightening to you. You may be afraid that you'll get overwhelmed or be stuck with the pain. But the truth is that emotions quickly come and go if you let them. If you don't try to fight, judge or beat yourself up over the feeling, you'll find that it soon fades, replaced by another emotion. It's only when you obsess over the feeling that it persists.

Step 3: Find new coping techniques

Self-harm is your way of dealing with feelings and difficult situations. So if you're going to stop, you need to have alternative ways of coping in place so you can respond differently when you start to feel like cutting or hurting yourself.

If you cut to express pain and intense emotions

⇨ Paint, draw or scribble on a big piece of paper with red ink or paint

⇨ Express your feelings in a journal

⇨ Compose a poem or song to say what you feel

⇨ Write down any negative feelings and then rip the paper up

⇨ Listen to music that expresses what you're feeling.

If you cut to calm and soothe yourself

⇨ Take a bath or hot shower

⇨ Pet or cuddle with a dog or cat

⇨ Wrap yourself in a warm blanket

⇨ Massage your neck, hands and feet

⇨ Listen to calming music.

If you cut because you feel disconnected and numb

⇨ Call a friend (you don't have to talk about self-harm)

⇨ Take a cold shower

⇨ Hold an ice cube in the crook of your arm or leg

⇨ Chew something with a very strong taste, like chilli peppers, peppermint or a grapefruit peel

⇨ Go online to a self-help website, chat room or message board.

If you cut to release tension or vent anger

⇨ Exercise vigorously – run, dance, skip or hit a punching bag

⇨ Punch a cushion or mattress or scream into your pillow

⇨ Squeeze a stress ball or squish play dough or clay

⇨ Rip something up (sheets of paper, a magazine)

⇨ Make some noise (play an instrument, bang on pots and pans).

Substitutes for the cutting sensation

⇨ Use a red felt tip pen to mark where you might usually cut

⇨ Rub ice across your skin where you might usually cut

⇨ Put rubber bands on wrists, arms or legs and snap them instead of cutting or hitting.

Source: The Mental Health Foundation, UK.

Professional treatment for cutting and self-harm

You may also need the help and support of a trained professional as you work to overcome the self-harm habit, so consider talking to a therapist. A therapist can help you develop new coping techniques and strategies to stop self-harming, while also helping you get to the root of why you cut or hurt yourself.

Remember, self-harm doesn't occur in a vacuum. It's an outward expression of inner pain – pain that often has its roots in early life. There is often a connection between self-harm and childhood trauma.

Self-harm may be your way of coping with feelings related to past abuse, flashbacks, negative feelings about your body or other traumatic memories. This may be the case even if you're not consciously aware of the connection.

Finding the right therapist

Finding the right therapist may take some time. It's very important that the therapist you choose has experience treating both trauma and self-injury. But the quality of the relationship with your therapist is equally important. Trust your instincts. If you don't feel safe, respected or understood, find another therapist.

There should be a sense of trust and warmth between you and your therapist. This therapist should be someone who accepts self-harm without condoning it, and who is willing to help you work towards stopping it at your own pace. You should feel at ease with him or her, even while talking through your most personal issues.

Helping a friend or family member who cuts or self-harms

Perhaps you've noticed suspicious injuries on someone close to you, or that person has confided to you that he or she is cutting. Whatever the case may be, you may be feeling unsure of yourself. What should you say? How can you help?

Deal with your own feelings. You may feel shocked, confused, or even disgusted by self-harming behaviours – and guilty about admitting these feelings. Acknowledging your feelings is an important first step towards helping your loved one.

Learn about the problem. The best way to overcome any discomfort or distaste you feel about self-harm is by learning about it. Understanding why your friend or family member is self-injuring can help you see the world from his or her eyes.

Don't judge. Avoid judgmental comments and criticism – they'll only make things worse. The first two tips will go a long way in helping you with this. Remember, the self-harming person already feels ashamed and alone.

Offer support, not ultimatums. It's only natural to want to help, but threats, punishments and ultimatums are counterproductive. Express your concern and let the person know that you're available whenever he or she wants to talk or needs support.

Encourage communication. Encourage your loved one to express whatever he or she is feeling, even if it's something you might be uncomfortable with. If the person hasn't told you about the self-harm, bring up the subject in a caring, non-confrontational way: 'I've noticed injuries on your body, and I want to understand what you're going through.'

If the self-harmer is a family member, especially if it is your child, prepare yourself to address difficulties in the family. This is not about blame, but rather about learning ways of dealing with problems and communicating better that can help the whole family.

⇨ The above information is reprinted with kind permission from Helpguide. Please visit www.helpguide.org for further information.

Treatments for self-harming

By Beth Morrisey

There is no single means of treatment that is guaranteed to work in all cases of self-harming or cases in which an individual inflicts behaviours such as cutting, burning, head banging, hair pulling and even poisoning on his or her own body. Instead, a combination of treatments geared towards protecting the self-harmer's physical and mental health is often employed to treat self-harmers and help them cease their injurious behaviours. If a self-harmer is in need of medical treatment, this will usually be organised first to guarantee that there is no threat to the individual's life. When the individual's physical health has stabilised, treatment then usually begins to address the individual's mental and/or emotional health as well. In severe cases, residential treatment may be encouraged so that the individual can receive care and attention around the clock. There are several institutions across the United Kingdom that can provide this type of treatment as needed.

Medical treatment

It has been estimated that up to 10% of admissions to hospital wards in the United Kingdom are the result of self-harming behaviours, although since cases of overdose and other substance abuse/misuse are often included in these counts the statistics do become a little blurred. If, however, a self-harmer hurts him or herself to such an extent that medical attention is needed, this medical care will be given before any other type of treatment is explored to address the root causes of self-harming. Cleaning and treating wounds and burns, and investigating for bruises, broken bones and/or tissue damage are common means of providing care for cases of self-harm. Most self-harming behaviours are not done with suicidal intent; however some hospitals may choose to keep individuals who have self-harmed under observation just to be safe. When the individual's physical health has stabilised, counselling and/or therapy is usually then encouraged.

Counselling

Self-harming is often related to conditions such as depression, low self-esteem, feelings of powerlessness and feelings of being overwhelmed. When the root cause of self-harming behaviours is actually emotional, then this basis must be addressed. Traditional counselling, sometimes known as talk therapy, allows those who engage in self-harming behaviours to talk through their emotions and their decisions to self-harm. The counsellor or therapist involved will likely be a source of support for the self-harmer, and a behaviour modification approach may be able to teach self-harmers how to make more healthy choices in the future. If clinical depression is diagnosed, medication may be prescribed, but there is no medication that simply stops self-harming behaviours.

Residential treatment

Both public and private residential facilities exist in the United Kingdom to help treat individuals who engage in self-harming behaviours. Though all types of self-harm are unhealthy, the individual involved will usually need to engage in these behaviours repeatedly for a long period of time, or engage in them to such an extent that there is a risk of long-term health effects or even death before residential treatment options are broached. The Cassel Hospital (Surrey), Althea Park Specialist Service (Gloucestershire) and the Crisis Recovery Unit, Bethlem Royal Hospital (Kent) are but a few of the institutions offering residential treatment for self-harmers.

11 June 2013

⇨ The above information is reprinted with kind permission from Teen Issues. Please visit www.teenissues.co.uk for further information.

Lack of mental health services for children leaves them at risk of suicide and self-harm

New mental health charity launches online counselling support for young people.

One in five children* have symptoms of depression, and almost a third (32%) have thought about or attempted suicide before they were 16. That's according to a report from the new mental health charity, MindFull being launched today by the team behind BeatBullying.

The new charity will give 11- to 17-year-olds immediate access to free online professional counselling support and advice. The launch is supported by Ed Miliband MP and clinical psychologist Professor Tanya Byron.

The report, _Alone with my thoughts_, includes a survey by YouGov of over 2,000 young people which reveals that nearly a third (29%) have self-harmed because they feel 'down'. Over half (52%) of those who had shown signs of depression as children felt let down by their experiences of mental health support. On average, those children who showed symptoms of depression and talked to more than one person, ended up speaking to people 22 times before they got help. Almost half (47%) of young people with depression never got the help they wanted.

Emma-Jane Cross, CEO and founder of MindFull (part of The BB Group) said: 'Too many children who try to speak out about the way they're feeling are being let down or simply ignored. It's unacceptable that so many are having to resort to harming themselves on purpose in order to cope, or worse still are thinking about ending their own lives. Early intervention is proven to help prevent adult mental health problems, so swift action must be taken now if we are to avoid a legacy of serious long-term mental illness.

'MindFull is a direct result of the feedback that we have been given by thousands of young people in the UK, who tell us they want the flexibility and convenience of an online service.'

MindFull will give children and teenagers the support of mental health professionals and enable them to mentor one another in a safe space. The charity will also educate young people about how to cope with mental health issues – providing information, advice and guidance, both online and through training in schools.

Negative thoughts and feelings have a huge impact on children's lives. The survey shows that over a third (39%) of children said they had found it hard to leave the house because they felt down, and almost one in five (18%) young people say they have felt constantly on edge in the last two weeks. Over a third (38%) of those who had showed signs of depression as children said they had run away from home. Jessica was 14 when she started to feel very down. She didn't tell anyone about the way she was feeling until she was 15, and even though she started to have suicidal thoughts it took her six months before she was able to talk to her mum and get help.

'People don't understand the effect that depression has on you – I hate it when people dismiss it as simply teenage angst. Some days I feel so low it can be a struggle to do things that I normally love, like reading and writing. We desperately need more education about mental health issues so young people can spot the signs early.

'My generation is constantly online – it's where we look for information and advice, which is why I think a site like MindFull will make an enormous difference to all the young people who feel like they have no one to turn to.'

Children are most likely to speak to their friends about mental health issues, underlining the importance of peer support. Of those that spoke to someone, most confided in a friend (57%), followed by parents (54%) and a face-to-face counsellor (32%). Just 2% of young people said medicine alone is the best way to treat mental health issues, and over two-thirds (68%) think that putting mental health services online would be an effective way to tackle mental health issues among young people.

Professor Tanya Byron, President of The BB Group and Chartered Clinical Psychologist said:

'Just as we look after our children's physical health, it's vital that we also offer support for their mental well-being. Children and young people are clearly not getting the help they need, that's why this new online support from MindFull is so important. Teenagers naturally look to the Internet as a source of information and advice, so that's where we need to be in order to help the hundreds of thousands of young people who are currently getting no support.'

The survey also reinforces the need for more information and training in schools. Nearly two-thirds of young people believe adding information on mental health to the national curriculum and training teachers would be effective ways to tackle the problem.

MindFull is calling for mental health to be embedded as a core theme in the national curriculum and for schools to provide access to counselling and mentor support for all young people who need it.

* All figures, unless otherwise stated, are from YouGov plc.

5 July 2013

⇨ The above information is reprinted with kind permission from MindFull. Please visit www.mindfull.org for further information. Or you can e-mail hello@mindfull.org and call 02087 682 166.

Self-harm: information and suggestions for school staff

The information and suggestions in this article are intended to give school staff ideas to support young people who harm themselves.

Risk factors for self-harm behaviour

Any of the following risk factors may make a young person vulnerable to self-harm:

Individual factors

⇨ low mood/anxiety

⇨ an existing psychological or developmental difficulty (e.g. Asperger syndrome, learning difficulty)

⇨ difficulty communicating

⇨ low self-esteem

⇨ poor problem-solving skills

⇨ hopelessness

⇨ impulsivity

⇨ drug or alcohol abuse

⇨ confusion about sexuality or feeling different/ unaccepted (e.g. if gay, lesbian or bisexual).

Family factors

⇨ unreasonable expectations

⇨ religious/ethnicity/cultural identity dilemmas or conflict

⇨ young carers' role within the family

⇨ domestic violence

⇨ neglect or abuse (physical, sexual or emotional)

⇨ poor parental relationships and arguments

⇨ depression, deliberate self-harm or suicide in the family.

Social factors

⇨ difficulty in making relationships/loneliness

⇨ persistent bullying or peer rejection

⇨ racism

⇨ homophobic attitudes or bullying of children who think they may be gay, lesbian or bisexual

⇨ easy availability of drugs, medication or other methods of self-harm.

Triggers for self-harm behaviour

A number of factors may trigger the self-harm incident:

⇨ family relationship difficulties (the most common trigger for younger adolescents)

⇨ difficulties with peer relationships, e.g. break up of relationship (the most common trigger for older adolescents)

⇨ bullying

⇨ significant trauma (e.g. bereavement, abuse)

⇨ self-harm behaviour in other students or in the media (contagion effect)

⇨ difficult times of the year (e.g. anniversaries)

⇨ trouble in school or with the police

⇨ feeling under pressure from families, school and peers to conform/achieve

⇨ exam pressure

⇨ times of change (e.g. parental separation/divorce).

Warning signs

There may be a change in behaviour of the young person which is associated with self-harm or other serious emotional difficulties:

⇨ changes in eating/sleeping habits

⇨ increased isolation from friends/family

⇨ changes in activity and mood (e.g. more, or less, irritable or aggressive than usual)

⇨ lowering of academic grades

- talking about self-harming or suicide
- abusing drugs or alcohol
- becoming socially withdrawn
- expressing feelings of failure, uselessness or loss of hope
- giving away possessions.

Examples of self-harming behaviour

- cutting
- taking an overdose of tablets
- swallowing hazardous materials or substances
- burning – either physically or chemically
- over/under medicating (e.g. misuse of paracetamol, insulin or thyroxine)
- punching/hitting/bruising
- hair pulling/skin picking/head banging
- high-risk behaviour, such as running in front of cars
- episodes of alcohol/drug abuse or over/under eating can at times be acts of deliberate self-harm.

Young people report they self-harm to:

- relieve tension
- feel alive inside
- gain control
- numb themselves
- comfort themselves
- vent anger
- relieve emotional distress or overwhelming feelings
- stop bad thoughts
- feel the warm blood
- see 'red'
- punish themselves
- replace emotional pain with physical pain.

What keeps self-harm going?

Once self-harm (particularly cutting) is established it may be difficult to stop. Self-harm can form a number of functions for the student and can become a way of coping.

Examples of functions include:

- reduction in tension (safety valve)
- distraction from problems
- form of escape
- outlet for anger and rage

- way of punishing self
- perceived way of taking control
- care-eliciting behaviour
- a means of getting identity with a peer group
- non-verbal communication.

It can also have suicidal intent.

The cycle of self-harm/cutting

When a person inflicts pain upon himself or herself the body responds by producing endorphins, a natural pain reliever that gives temporary relief or a feeling of peace. The addictive nature of this feeling can make self-harm difficult to stop.

Young people that self-harm still feel pain, but some say the physical pain is easier to stand than the emotional/mental pain that led to the self-harm initially.

February 2011

- The above information is reprinted with kind permission from Children's Community Health Partnership, North Bristol NHS Trust. Please visit www.nbt.nhs.uk for further information.

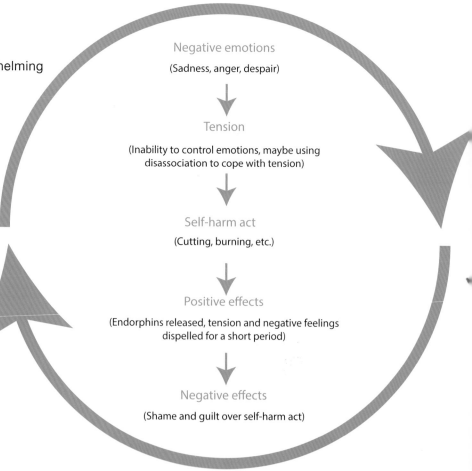

Negative emotions
(Sadness, anger, despair)

Tension
(Inability to control emotions, maybe using disassociation to cope with tension)

Self-harm act
(Cutting, burning, etc.)

Positive effects
(Endorphins released, tension and negative feelings dispelled for a short period)

Negative effects
(Shame and guilt over self-harm act)

'Controlled self-harm' policy leaves school under investigation

By Cara Acred

Unsted Park School in Surrey is under investigation following the revelation that they implemented a controlled self-harm policy, providing sterilised razors to a pupil at the school.

Unsted Park is part of the Priory Group, and provides education for students aged seven to 19 who have Asperger syndrome and autism.

The self-harm policy is thought to have been designed in collaboration with a female student's mother and involved staff escorting the student to the bathroom and waiting outside while she carried out self-harm in a 'safe and controlled manner'. Staff were told they should check on the student every two minutes, then dress and clean the wound afterwards.

The Principal and Headteacher of the school are both likely to undergo a professional conduct hearing and are facing allegations of 'unacceptable professional conduct'.

The controlled self-harm policy has now been abandoned, and several staff members are believed to have protested against its implementation.

A spokesman for the Priory Group commented: 'This was a short-term, local procedure introduced by the headteacher and school principal who genuinely believed it was in the best interests of the pupil.'

While the Teaching Agency said they were unable to comment during the on-going investigation, a spokesperson from the charity Selfharm.co.uk said that controlled self-harm has proved successful in some areas, but that this should only be done under the correct supervision. They also warned that introducing such a policy and then taking it away could have very damaging consequences if it was not replaced with something else to help the student cope.

According to the BBC News, the incident occurred in January 2012 and the Department for Education became aware of the incident in December 2012.

6 November 2013

⇨ The above article was written by Cara Acred for Independence Educational Publishers.

mental health foundation

Suicide

Around 4,400 people end their own lives in England each year – that's one death every two hours – and at least ten times that number attempt suicide.

Around 75% of suicides are men and in almost all cultures, the suicide rate rises with age. The highest rates of suicide in the UK are among people aged over 75 and it remains a common cause of death in men under the age of 35.

Risk factors

Certain factors are known to be associated with increased risk of suicide. These include:

⇨ drug and alcohol misuse

⇨ unemployment

⇨ social isolation

⇨ poverty

⇨ poor social conditions

⇨ imprisonment

⇨ violence

⇨ family breakdown.

People with a diagnosed mental health condition are at particular risk. Around 90% of suicide victims suffer from a psychiatric disorder at the time of their death.

Those at the highest risk of suicide are people suffering from alcoholism, clinical depression or schizophrenia. Previous suicide attempts are also an indication of particular risk. Up to 20% of survivors try again within a year, and as a group they are 100 times more likely to go on to complete suicide than those who have never attempted suicide.

For young people, bullying, family turmoil, mental health problems, unemployment and a family history of suicide can play a part in increasing the risk of suicide. Amongst the young, 80% of suicides are male, and one in three young people who take their lives are intoxicated at the time of death.

For older people, poverty, poor quality housing, social isolation, depression and physical health problems are factors which can increase the risk of suicide. Over 1,000 men aged 50+ end their own lives every year in England and Wales.

Prevention

Feeling suicidal is often a temporary state of mind. If appropriate and timely help and emotional support is offered to people who are experiencing deep unhappiness and distress, this can reduce the risk of them choosing to end their own life.

Following a focused campaign in recent years, numbers of suicides among younger men aged 25 to 34 – previously the highest – have fallen.

Attempts at suicide are often preceded by certain signs. These can include evidence of deliberate self-harm and the person in question expressing their thoughts in the year before the act to relatives, partners, peers or professionals. These offer potential opportunities to intervene and save lives.

Despite this, three-quarters of all people who end their own lives are not in contact with mental health services.

Prevention of suicide is not the exclusive responsibility of any one sector of society. Schools can create cultures in which young people feel it is healthy to talk through emotional and other difficulties. General practitioners can restrict the number of tablets prescribed to those at risk of overdose. Accident and Emergency staff can ensure all young people who have attempted suicide receive specialist mental health assessment. And each of us can pay close attention to the overall mental health of our loved ones to reduce the risks of them taking their lives.

Recovery from a suicide attempt

The attitudes we hold toward people who attempt to take their lives can influence the course of their condition. The isolation that suicidal people feel can be reinforced by a judgemental approach in which their behaviour is viewed as manipulative or selfish. By stepping beyond our personal assumptions, and showing care and respect for the people behind the behaviours, we can help them talk about their feelings and help prevent suicide taking place.

⇨ The above information is reprinted with kind permission from the Mental Health Foundation. Please visit www.mentalhealth.org.uk for further information.

Suicide rates are on the increase, recession possible factor

More needs to be done to help mentally ill people, as the number who commit suicide is on the increase, figures suggest.

There were 1,333 suicides among mental health patients in England in 2011 – up from 1,175 in 2010, according to new provisional statistics.

Recently, suicide and mental illness were thrust into the spotlight after Stephen Fry revealed he attempted suicide last year using pills and vodka.

Researchers from the National Confidential Inquiry into Suicide and Homicide by People with Mental Illness said that 'current economic difficulties' are likely to be a contributory factor to the increase, with debts, housing and employment as driving concerns.

Professor Louis Appleby, director of the National Confidential Inquiry, said: 'The increase in suicide among mental health patients is in line with an increase in the general population and is mostly likely due to the current economic circumstances.

'Although these are only early indicators, it would suggest services should try to address the economic difficulties of patients who might be at risk of suicide.

'Ensuring patients receive advice on debts, housing and employment could make a difference, while improvements in home treatment should now become a priority for suicide prevention. Particular caution is needed with home treatment for patients who live alone or are reluctant to accept treatment.'

Janet Davies, executive director of nursing and service delivery for the Royal College of Nursing added: 'Any suicide is a personal tragedy, and one whose effects can be felt by families for many years. Working to help people at risk of suicide is uniquely challenging, but the progress which has been made in preventing suicide by inpatients shows that the compassion and commitment of mental health staff does make a difference.

'Nurses will be very concerned about the rising number of people who are committing suicide while being treated at home. The reasons for this are highly complex, and the Government, NHS and clinicians must work together to understand as much as possible about how these tragedies can be prevented.

'Sadly, we know from past experience that many people do reach a crisis point in their mental health after a number of years of economic downturn. The mental health of the population provides a significant and urgent impetus for efforts to improve economic stability across the board. It also makes it more important than ever that services are available to meet the extra demand generated by the economic downturn.'

The research, conducted by experts from the University of Manchester, found that the number of people murdered by mentally ill patients was 33 in England in 2010 – the lowest figure since 1997.

For advice or help, or if you have been affected by suicide, visit the Samaritans website.

4 July 2013

⇨ The above information is reprinted with kind permission from *The Huffington Post UK*. Please visit www.huffingtonpost.co.uk for further information.

Suicide prevention

A suicidal person may not ask for help, but that doesn't mean that help isn't wanted. Most people who commit suicide don't want to die – they just want to stop hurting. Suicide prevention starts with recognising the warning signs and taking them seriously. If you think a friend or family member is considering suicide, you might be afraid to bring up the subject. But talking openly about suicidal thoughts and feelings can save a life.

Understanding and preventing suicide

The World Health Organization estimates that approximately one million people die each year from suicide. What drives so many individuals to take their own lives? To those not in the grips of suicidal depression and despair, it's difficult to understand what drives so many individuals to take their own lives. But a suicidal person is in so much pain that he or she can see no other option.

Suicide is a desperate attempt to escape suffering that has become unbearable. Blinded by feelings of self-loathing, hopelessness and isolation, a suicidal person can't see any way of finding relief except through death. But despite their desire for the pain to stop, most suicidal people are deeply conflicted about ending their own lives. They wish there was an alternative to committing suicide, but they just can't see one.

Warning signs of suicide

Most suicidal individuals give warning signs or signals of their intentions. The best way to prevent suicide is to recognise these warning signs and know how to respond if you spot them. If you believe that a friend or family member is suicidal, you can play a role in suicide prevention by pointing out the alternatives, showing that you care and getting a doctor or psychologist involved.

Major warning signs for suicide include talking about killing or harming oneself, talking or writing a lot about death or dying and seeking out things that could be used in a suicide attempt, such as weapons and drugs. These signals are even more dangerous if the person has a mood disorder such as depression or bipolar disorder, suffers from alcohol dependence, has previously attempted suicide or has a family history of suicide.

A more subtle but equally dangerous warning sign of suicide is hopelessness. Studies have found that hopelessness is a strong predictor of suicide. People who feel hopeless may talk about 'unbearable' feelings, predict a bleak future and state that they have nothing to look forward to.

Other warning signs that point to a suicidal mind frame include dramatic mood swings or sudden personality changes, such as going from outgoing to withdrawn or well-behaved to rebellious. A suicidal person may also lose interest in day-to-day activities, neglect his or her appearance and show big changes in eating or sleeping habits.

Suicide prevention tip one: speak up if you're worried

If you spot the warning signs of suicide in someone you care about, you may wonder if it's a good idea to say anything. What if you're wrong? What if the person gets angry? In such situations, it's natural to feel uncomfortable or afraid. But anyone who talks about suicide or shows other warning signs needs immediate help – the sooner the better.

Talking to a person about suicide

Talking to a friend or family member about their suicidal thoughts and feelings can be extremely difficult for anyone. But if you're unsure whether someone is suicidal, the best way to find out is to ask. You can't make a person suicidal by showing that you care. In fact, giving a suicidal person the opportunity to express his or her feelings can provide relief from loneliness and pent-up negative feelings, and may prevent a suicide attempt.

Ways to start a conversation about suicide:

⇨ I have been feeling concerned about you lately.

⇨ Recently, I have noticed some differences in you and wondered how you are doing.

⇨ I wanted to check in with you because you haven't seemed yourself lately.

Questions you can ask:

⇨ When did you begin feeling like this?

⇨ Did something happen that made you start feeling this way?

⇨ How can I best support you right now?

⇨ Have you thought about getting help?

What you can say that helps:

⇨ You are not alone in this. I'm here for you.

⇨ You may not believe it now, but the way you're feeling will change.

⇨ I may not be able to understand exactly how you feel, but I care about you and want to help.

When you want to give up, tell yourself you will hold off for just one more day, hour, minute – whatever you can manage.

When talking to a suicidal person

Do:

⇨ Be yourself. Let the person know you care, that he/she is not alone. The right words are often unimportant. If you are concerned, your voice and manner will show it.

⇨ Listen. Let the suicidal person unload despair, ventilate anger. No matter how negative the conversation seems, the fact that it exists is a positive sign.

⇨ Be sympathetic, non-judgemental, patient, calm, accepting. Your friend or family member is doing the right thing by talking about his/her feelings.

⇨ Offer hope. Reassure the person that help is available and that the suicidal feelings are temporary. Let the person know that his or her life is important to you.

⇨ If the person says things like, 'I'm so depressed, I can't go on,' ask the question: 'Are you having thoughts of suicide?' You are not putting ideas in their head, you are showing that you are concerned, that you take them seriously and that it's OK for them to share their pain with you.

But don't:

⇨ Argue with the suicidal person. Avoid saying things like: 'You have so much to live for,' 'Your suicide will hurt your family,' or 'Look on the bright side.'

⇨ Act shocked, lecture on the value of life, or say that suicide is wrong.

⇨ Promise confidentiality. Refuse to be sworn to secrecy. A life is at stake and you may need to speak to a mental health professional in order to keep the suicidal person safe. If you promise to keep your discussions secret, you may have to break your word.

⇨ Offer ways to fix their problems, or give advice, or make them feel like they have to justify their suicidal feelings. It is not about how bad the problem is, but how badly it's hurting your friend or loved one.

⇨ Blame yourself. You can't 'fix' someone's depression. Your loved one's happiness, or lack thereof, is not your responsibility.

Adapted from: Metanoia.org

Suicide prevention tip two: respond quickly in a crisis

If a friend or family member tells you that he or she is thinking about death or suicide, it's important to evaluate the immediate danger the person is in. Those at the highest risk for committing suicide in the near future have a specific suicide PLAN, the MEANS to carry out the plan, a TIME SET for doing it and an INTENTION to do it.

The following questions can help you assess the immediate risk for suicide:

⇨ Do you have a suicide plan? (PLAN)

⇨ Do you have what you need to carry out your plan (pills, gun, etc.)? (MEANS)

⇨ Do you know when you would do it? (TIME SET)

⇨ Do you intend to commit suicide? (INTENTION)

If a suicide attempt seems imminent, call a local crisis centre, dial 911, or take the person to an emergency room. Remove guns, drugs, knives and other potentially lethal objects from the vicinity but do not, under any circumstances, leave a suicidal person alone.

Suicide prevention tip three: offer help and support

If a friend or family member is suicidal, the best way to help is by offering an empathetic, listening ear. Let your loved one know that he or she is not alone and that you care. Don't take responsibility, however, for making your loved one well. You can offer support, but you can't get better for a suicidal person. He or she has to make a personal commitment to recovery.

It takes a lot of courage to help someone who is suicidal. Witnessing a loved one dealing with thoughts about ending his or her own life can stir up many difficult emotions. As you're helping a suicidal person, don't forget to take care of yourself. Find someone that you trust – a friend, family member, clergyman or counsellor – to talk to about your feelings and get support of your own.

Helping a suicidal person:

⇨ Get professional help. Do everything in your power to get a suicidal person the help he or she needs. Call a crisis line for advice and referrals. Encourage the person to see a mental health professional, help locate a treatment facility or take them to a doctor's appointment.

⇨ Follow-up on treatment. If the doctor prescribes medication, make sure your friend or loved one takes it as directed. Be aware of possible side effects and be sure to notify the physician if the person seems to be getting worse. It often takes time and persistence to find the medication or therapy that's right for a particular person.

⇨ Be proactive. Those contemplating suicide often don't believe they can be helped, so you may have to be more proactive at offering assistance. Saying, 'Call me if you need anything' is too vague. Don't wait for the person to call you or even to return your calls. Drop by, call again, invite the person out.

⇨ Encourage positive lifestyle changes, such as a healthy diet, plenty of sleep and getting out in the sun or into nature for at least 30 minutes each day. Exercise is also extremely important as it releases endorphins, relieves stress and promotes emotional well-being.

⇨ Make a safety plan. Help the person develop a set of steps he or she promises to follow during a suicidal crisis. It should identify any triggers that may lead to a suicidal crisis, such as an anniversary of a loss, alcohol or stress from relationships. Also include contact numbers for the person's doctor or therapist, as well as friends and family members who will help in an emergency.

⇨ Remove potential means of suicide, such as pills, knives, razors or firearms. If the person is likely to take an overdose, keep medications locked away or give out only as the person needs them.

⇨ Continue your support over the long haul. Even after the immediate suicidal crisis has passed, stay in touch with the person, periodically checking in or dropping by. Your support is vital to ensure your friend or loved one remains on the recovery track.

Common suicide risk factors include:

⇨ Mental illness

⇨ Alcoholism or drug abuse

⇨ Previous suicide attempts

⇨ Family history of suicide

⇨ Terminal illness or chronic pain

⇨ Recent loss or stressful life event

⇨ Social isolation and loneliness

⇨ History of trauma or abuse.

Suicide in teens and older adults

In addition to the general risk factors for suicide, both teenagers and older adults are at a higher risk of suicide.

Suicide in teens

Teenage suicide is a serious and growing problem. The teenage years can be emotionally turbulent and stressful. Teenagers face pressures to succeed and fit in. They may struggle with self-esteem issues, self-doubt and feelings of alienation. For some, this leads to suicide. Depression is also a major risk factor for teen suicide.

Other risk factors for teenage suicide include:

⇨ Childhood abuse

⇨ Recent traumatic event

⇨ Lack of a support network

⇨ Availability of a gun

⇨ Hostile social or school environment

⇨ Exposure to other teen suicides.

Suicide warning signs in teens

Additional warning signs that a teen may be considering suicide:

⇨ Change in eating and sleeping habits

⇨ Withdrawal from friends, family and regular activities

⇨ Violent or rebellious behaviour, running away

⇨ Drug and alcohol use

⇨ Unusual neglect of personal appearance

⇨ Persistent boredom, difficulty concentrating or a decline in the quality of schoolwork

⇨ Frequent complaints about physical symptoms, often related to emotions, such as stomach aches, headaches, fatigue, etc.

⇨ Not tolerating praise or rewards.

Source: American Academy of Child & Adolescent Psychiatry.

Suicide in the elderly

The highest suicide rates of any age group occur among persons aged 65 years and older. One contributing factor is depression in the elderly that is undiagnosed and untreated.

Other risk factors for suicide in the elderly include:

⇨ Recent death of a loved one

⇨ Physical illness, disability or pain

⇨ Isolation and loneliness

⇨ Major life changes, such as retirement

⇨ Loss of independence

⇨ Loss of sense of purpose.

Suicide warning signs in older adults

Additional warning signs that an elderly person may be contemplating suicide:

⇨ Reading material about death and suicide

⇨ Disruption of sleep patterns

⇨ Increased alcohol or prescription drug use

⇨ Failure to take care of self or follow medical orders

⇨ Stockpiling medications

⇨ Sudden interest in firearms

⇨ Social withdrawal or elaborate good-byes

⇨ Rush to complete or revise a will.

July 2013

⇨ The above information is reprinted with kind permission from HelpGuide. Please visit www.helpguide.org for further information.

Level of suicide risk

Low: Some suicidal thoughts. No suicide plan. Says he or she won't commit suicide.

Moderate: Suicidal thoughts. Vague plan that isn't very lethal. Says he or she won't commit suicide.

High: Suicidal thoughts. Specific plan that is highly lethal. Says he or she won't commit suicide.

Severe: Suicidal thoughts. Specific plan that is highly lethal. Says he or she will commit suicide.

Dos and don'ts

If you have noticed a pattern of behaviours in someone you know that is consistent with some of the risk factors and warning signs, it is time to take action. Here are some things you should and should not do when you think someone may be at risk of suicide:

Remain calm

Though you may be shocked and overwhelmed, it is important to try to stay relaxed. By remaining calm, you are creating a comfortable atmosphere for the person who is suicidal to open up to you and reach out for your help. Do not give up hope or begin to panic. If an individual is opening up to you, he or she must trust you and feel comfortable with you. Do not doubt yourself in the situation. It is important that the person have someone with them, so make sure to not leave him or her alone. Remember, what this person really needs right now is a friend.

Be prepared to talk about suicide

Four out of five completed suicides gave clear warning signs before the attempt. While death is an uncomfortable subject for many people, it is important to be able to talk about it openly and honestly. There should be no fear in talking to someone about suicide. By discussing it, you are not putting the idea in their head or increasing the likelihood of suicidal behaviour. An open discussion can help decrease some of the anxiety experienced by a suicidal person and come as a relief to them that someone else cares and wants to help them. Talking about suicide can help them see the other options they have. Further, asking them if they are suicidal can be helpful because some people view this question as permission to feel the way they do, making it easier for them to open up.

When talking to a person who may be suicidal, it is important not to minimise or dismiss their problems. Instead, try to provide them with reassurance. Be sure to acknowledge their fear, sadness and other emotions, and tell them you care about them and want to help them. Keep from encouraging feelings of guilt or being judgemental.

Since people who are contemplating suicide feel so alone and helpless, the most important thing to do if you think a friend or loved one is suicidal is to communicate with him or her openly and frequently. Make it clear that you care; stress your willingness to listen. Your first question should be whether or not he or she is having suicidal thoughts. If the answer is yes, then ask the individual if he or she has a plan of how to do it. If the answer is yes, ask if he or she has obtained whatever is needed to do it, and if so, if a time has been determined. Getting the answers to these questions can help you evaluate the mind-set of the person and get him or her the necessary help.

Be prepared to act

When a suicidal individual wants to open up to you, don't be afraid to get involved and take action to get them help.

If someone is suicidal, he or she must not be left alone. Try to get the person to seek help immediately from his or her doctor or the nearest emergency room, or call 999. It is also important to limit the person's access to firearms, medications or other lethal items that could lead to suicide.

Do not try to play the hero

Though it is important to act immediately, it is better not to act alone. Helping a suicidal person is not easy. It can take a lot of time and energy and bring forth an array of emotions. Having the support of others can help you help someone else. Additionally, you should never attempt to physically take away a weapon. You do not want to put yourself in a dangerous situation, nor do you want to aggravate the suicidal individual.

HELP ME TO HELP YOU!

Do not promise confidentiality

Though an individual may ask you to guarantee confidentiality, try to avoid making this promise, and be prepared to break it if you do. Keeping an individual's promise is not as important as saving a life. Though the person may be hurt and angry initially, you must remember that he or she is unable to think clearly right now, and realise it may take time to begin to return your relationship to what it was.

⇨ The above information is reprinted with kind permission from The Jason Foundation. Please visit www. jasonfoundation.com for further information.

© The Jason Foundation 2013

Making sense of suicide

Suicide is a highly emotive subject, still often treated as taboo in most cultures. This means that even though it is fairly common, of all the forms of depressed thinking, suicidal thinking is least likely to be aired, discussed and critically evaluated.

Deadly tunnel vision

Isolation and painful despair in conjunction with depressed thinking habits make for a very risky combination. Suicidal thinking often arises out of hopelessness about being able to overcome difficult life problems. When someone is desperate for relief from suffering, yet stuck in tunnel vision at the bottom of the depression habit spiral, they are less able to apply problem-solving skills and are vulnerable to the deadly over-simplification of suicidal thinking. The taboo over discussing suicide also means that thinking about suicide can leave someone feeling very isolated and alone.

So how do we make sense of suicide?

Several different paths of thought can lead in the direction of suicide. All are distorted by the narrowed perspective of depressed thinking habits:

'How bad am I feeling?'

People often first think about suicide not so much as an immediate option, but more as a kind of 'barometer' to measure how bad they're feeling. When you are feeling very low, it can seem comforting to recognise that you do not feel quite low enough to commit suicide. This is a very risky habit, because repetition of the thought brings a seemingly comforting familiarity and dulls the initial instinctive recoil from danger.

'Am I a coward or a hero?'

Debate over whether suicide is heroic or cowardly is another irrelevant over-simplification. This kind of all-or-nothing thinking diverts attention from more complex solutions to the problems which have led to the suicidal thinking in the first place.

'I've got to sort it out on my own'

An over-emphasis on individualism, common in western cultures, creates barriers to help-seeking. Over-valuing 'independence' means that when someone can't find their own solution to their problems suicide becomes the only 'answer'. Yet many people can be, and have been, helped to survive suicidal thinking and overcome depression.

'Won't they be better off without me?'

One angle on suicide focuses on its self-sacrificial aspect, not wanting to be a burden. Yet the distorted perspective of believing that 'they'll be better off without me' tends to be greeted with stunned bewilderment and terrible pain by those who will supposedly be 'better off'. The anguish of a parent who has lost a child to suicide is almost indescribable.

'I'll show them!'

For some, the desire to cause this pain and bewilderment, or at least to have people take them seriously, is a strong motivation. This is the ultimate in cutting off your nose to spite your face – again an over-simplified solution to the complex problem of engaging in meaningful relationships.

Copycat suicide

It is an unfortunate phenomenon that one suicide can sometimes seem to create a kind of domino effect, sparking off a series of suicides in the affected community. More commonly, a suicide in the community is shocking enough to jolt support networks into action for others.

'What's the point to life anyway?'

Pervading cynicism in modern societies creates a strongly depression-inducing cultural context. Cynicism denigrates all that is constructive and hopeful and drains away the meaning from life. Depression and suicidal thinking thrive in the vacuum left when people stop investing hope in their lives.

To be or not to be?

The famous 'To be or not to be...?' speech in Shakespeare's play Hamlet reminds us of another aspect to thinking about suicide. It reflects the strong tradition in many cultures of contemplating death as a way of bringing into focus the value of life.

Depression and the meaning of life

Pain, suffering and the inevitability of death are profoundly difficult issues not just for individuals but for all of humanity.

Surviving suicidal thoughts

A risky habit

Suicidal intentions are prompted by a desperate need for relief from intensely painful feelings. Surviving suicidal thoughts is about learning how to find relief without resorting to suicide.

Simply having suicidal thoughts does not mean you will act on them.

However, the habit of repeatedly thinking about suicide is a risky one. Repetition brings a sense of falsely comforting familiarity. It dulls the instinctive recoil from danger. Though it may be difficult, hold on to the belief that there ARE ways to resist depression and find relief.

Making a safety plan

A safety plan helps you plan ahead for the times when you may feel particularly low and at risk of acting on your suicidal thoughts. It is a way to personalise and summarise the possible strategies for taking care of yourself.

A safety plan supports your healthier self – the bit of you that wants to hold on and survive – when things are hard and you are feeling overwhelmed. The strategies listed here offer a solid foundation for creating a safety plan and for working towards breaking the suicidal thinking habit:

Make a commitment to yourself

When you notice thoughts of suicide, challenge the self-bullying habit and make a commitment to taking care of yourself as best you possibly can for the moment. Remind yourself to follow your safety plan if you have made one.

Attend to your self-care needs

Suicidal thoughts arise as a result of deeply painful feelings of despair and hopelessness. Recognise the pain you are feeling as something which needs a compassionate and caring response. Practise constructive ways to take care of yourself when you are feeling this way.

Tell someone how you're feeling

Tell someone else how you are feeling or get someone to be with you. Be prepared for non-professionals to be shocked by what you tell them, and don't expect a 'perfect' response – it is always better to make human contact than to stay isolated and alone with your thoughts.

Reduce the risks

Protect yourself from impulsively acting on your thoughts by putting dangerous objects out of immediate reach. Preferably give pills, weapons, etc. to someone else for safe-keeping, but even putting them in a locked or inaccessible place makes it a little harder to act impulsively.

Plan to get professional help

It is unreasonable to see suicide as the only solution if you haven't sought any professional help for your depression and suicidal thinking. Doctors and counsellors help many people move on from depression and get appropriate help. You may need to challenge yourself about what's stopping you getting help.

Check medication side effects

Be aware that some anti-depressant medication can increase the risk of suicidal thinking, especially when you first start taking them. Also, when the medication first starts taking effect it can increase your energy and motivation before improving your mood, increasing the risk of acting on suicidal thoughts. Talk to your doctor about the risks and be extra vigilant with other strategies for keeping yourself safe.

Check alcohol and drugs

Both alcohol and drugs tend to reduce your inhibitions and make it more likely you could do something you will regret the next day. Check your alcohol/drug consumption and try to cut down. Try not to drink alone or to end up alone after drinking.

Minimise time spent alone

Depression and suicidal thinking thrive in isolation. Try to minimise time spent alone in your room – take work to the library, ask friends to be with you at vulnerable times, make plans ahead for weekends and other lonelier times, generally work on building your support networks.

Give yourself small goals

Each evening set yourself small tasks or goals for the next day. It can be something as simple as watching a certain TV programme. Or set yourself another task as soon as you have completed one. Just knowing you can still do things you set for yourself despite feeling low can help combat depression.

Identify depressed thinking habits

Suicidal thinking is the ultimate all-or-nothing thinking habit, and the culmination of other habits of depressed thinking which intensify the depression habit spiral. Learn more about identifying and challenging depressed thinking, particularly self-bullying.

Start breaking the suicidal thinking habit

We can't stop thoughts from entering our heads, but we can stop actively inviting them in. Try to stop using thoughts of suicide as a barometer for how bad you are feeling. Use self-soothing or distraction techniques when you notice thoughts about suicide bothering you, or practise other techniques for challenging depressed thinking.

Understand some of the reasons for suicidal thinking

Because suicide is such a taboo, you may not be aware of how common it is for people to think about suicide and of the various general reasons for suicidal thinking.

Work on rebuilding meaning in your life

Depression works to drain assumed meaning out of life and challenges us to take responsibility for making our lives meaningful. Challenge the cynicism or perfectionism which may be preventing you from embracing hopeful or constructive ideals and goals for your life.

⇨ The above material is from studentsagainstdepression. org, a project of the Charlie Waller Memorial Trust. Intellectual property rights for the site are owned by Dr Denise Meyer. We are grateful to the Trust for allowing us to use their material.

© Students Against Depression

Mental health and suicide: how to talk to pupils about a topical issue

One in four people will experience mental illness at some stage in their lives. Data show that this issue is one that teachers in particular need to be aware of: the UK charity YoungMinds cites Office for National Statistics data saying that one in ten children of school age suffers from a diagnosable mental health disorder.

The topic of mental ill health has been a high-profile one this week; Michael Jackson's teenage daughter Paris has been hospitalised after a suicide attempt, while a few days ago television star and mental health campaigner Stephen Fry went public about a bid to end his own life last year.

While some may feel comfortable covering the issue of mental illness in the classroom, suicide is an extremely emotive and sensitive subject that can be difficult to broach. However, with two prominent stories in the news, it is possible that some students may come to teaching staff with questions about mental illness and suicide.

Much of the response to questions from students on this subject should depend on your knowledge of the individual child, their emotional intelligence and their personal circumstances, but we hope that these general tips will help you in formulating answers to any challenging questions that may come your way.

The most important thing to know is that talking about suicide will not put suicidal thoughts into anyone's head. In fact, talking about suicide and the issues surrounding it can prove incredibly helpful for people.

One of the most common questions about dying by suicide concerns what that actually means. Younger students may not have come across the word before, while older students may not have a full understanding of what it means. One starting point may be to ask a child to explain what they believe the word means and what they have heard about it before. This way, you can dispel any myths and/or misconceptions they may have.

Phrases that you can use to explain suicide include 'killing him/herself' or 'took their own life' – try to avoid using euphemisms such as 'gone away' or 'gone to sleep' as this can be confusing and frightening for children.

Explaining why people choose to take their own life can also be a tricky subject to negotiate. Child psychologist Polly Dunn suggests a possible approach in her blog: 'With kids, I have often compared it to a seemingly healthy person dying suddenly from a heart attack. Although they looked healthy on the outside, something was going wrong on the inside that we did not know about.'

Samaritans, a charity that provides emotional support to people who are in distress, also gives guidelines for appropriate language to use when talking about suicide attempts. It discourages referring to 'successful' or 'unsuccessful/failed' suicide attempts because of the connotations of those words. Talking about a 'victim' of suicide or someone 'committing suicide' is also best avoided, because of the implication in those words that suicide is an illegal or immoral act.

If you are worried about a child's mental health and you would like ideas for how to start a conversation with them, Samaritans has produced a helpful booklet on schools and suicide, which includes details of organisations that you can refer children to if appropriate.

In addition, the National Association of School Psychologists in the US has put together a list of warning signs of youth suicide, which may prove useful.

If you are worried about your own, or a colleague's, well-being, have a look at the TES Connect collection on managing your mental health, which has resources, articles and helpline information for teaching staff.

Starting difficult conversations: advice from Samaritans

If you're worried about a young person, try to get them to talk to you.

⇨ Often people want to talk, but won't speak until someone asks how they are. Try asking open questions, like: 'What happened about...', 'Tell me about...', 'How do you feel about...'

⇨ Repeat back what they say to show you understand, and ask more questions.

⇨ Focus on their feelings instead of trying to solve the problem – it can be of more help and shows you care.

⇨ Respect what they tell you. Sometimes it's easy to want to try and fix a young person's problems, or give them advice. Try and let them make their own decisions.

TES teacher tip: it is important to alert the young person to the fact that you may not be able to keep what they tell you a secret if you believe them to be at risk.

Samaritans can be contacted 24 hours a day for confidential, non-judgemental emotional support.

Telephone: 08457 90 90 90.

7 June 2013

⇨ The above information is reprinted with kind permission from TES. Please visit www.tes.co.uk for further information.

Children becoming increasingly unhappy, report warns

Young teenagers are becoming increasingly unhappy, with growing concerns about school, their appearance and the amount of choice and freedom they have, a report has warned.

By Victoria Ward

The study, published by the Children's Society following interviews with 42,000 children aged between eight and 17, found that after a long period of gradual increase, children's happiness began to stall in 2008 and had more recently been in decline.

Experts warned that such well-being and mental health issues were too often dismissed as teenage angst, creating a culture of misunderstanding and ignorance.

Emma-Jane Cross, founder of MindFull, the mental health charity for children and young people, said: 'This damaging attitude can no longer continue when so many are desperately unhappy and struggling with serious issues including self-harm and suicidal thoughts.

'Instead of a nation where young people are supported to be healthy, happy and fulfilled, we have a culture of stigma, misunderstanding and ignorance. Our young people deserve better.'

The Good Childhood Report found that teenagers aged 14 and 15 had the lowest satisfaction levels, with 15 per cent found to have 'low well-being' compared to just four per cent of eight-year-olds.

It warned that although many young people did not meet the criteria for mental health problems, they were nevertheless 'substantially unhappy' with their lives.

Those teenagers were more likely to have low academic motivation, poor quality relationships with their family and feel as though they have a lot less money than their friends.

One interviewee said: 'I know a lot of people who kind of feel forced to wear certain clothes because they're in the "in set" and they could get rejected.'

Another said: 'I wear what I want to wear but sometimes I do get people looking at me but I don't really mind because it's a free choice and I don't mind if people stare. They can do what they want.'

Perceived levels of choice, autonomy and freedom were found to be directly linked to satisfaction levels, dropping between the ages of eight and 15 before rising at 16 and 17.

The study found that British children did not fare well in comparison with many developed nations, echoing the conclusions of a recent UNICEF report that ranked the UK 14th out of 29 countries on children's life satisfaction.

Matthew Reed, chief executive of The Children's Society, described the drop in children's happiness as 'incredibly worrying'.

He said: 'These startling findings show that we should be paying particular attention to improving the happiness of this country's teenagers.

> **'We have a culture of stigma, misunderstanding and ignorance. Our young people deserve better'**

'These findings clearly show that we can't simply dismiss their low well-being as inevitable "teen grumpiness". They are facing very real problems we can all work to solve, such as not feeling safe at home, being exposed to family conflict or being bullied.

'It is so important that we all, from governments to professionals to parents, talk, listen and take seriously what children and teenagers are telling us.'

Psychologist Dr Linda Papadopoulos said of the report: 'Interestingly, this report suggests that, when it comes to well-being, 14- and 15-year-olds fare worse. It is so important that we don't simply dismiss this dip as an inevitable part of growing up, that it is just teenagers being teenagers. We really must talk to this generation and listen to what they have to say.'

Lucie Russell, director of campaigns and policy at well-being and mental health charity YoungMinds, said: 'These findings must not be dismissed as simply an inevitable part of growing up.

'Last year our parents' helpline received a record number of calls from parents concerned about the mental health or well-being of their child. We must take notice of these warning signs and act if we are not to see children increasingly struggling to cope.'

22 July 2013

⇨ The above information is reprinted with kind permission from *The Telegraph*. Please visit www.telegraph.co.uk for further information.

What I'm thinking about... teen suicides in fiction

Young adult novels about teenage suicide are on the increase, but is it a taboo too far?

By Julia Eccleshare

Two teenagers commit suicide; bewildered, their friends desperate try to get their lives back on track. Anger, guilt and sheer overwhelming misery fuel the next long phase of their own adolescences, which are overshadowed by the question: 'why?' It is happening all too horribly often. Luckily, this time it is fiction.

In teen novels, as in life, suicide is becoming more common, as a new generation of writers for young adults confronts what has previously been seen as the last taboo.

Some of them turned up at Edinburgh this week. Cat Clarke introduced *Undone*, about a teenager who kills himself after an explicit video revealing that he is gay is circulated among his friends. In *Kite Spirit* by Sita Brahmachari, a 'perfect' student commits suicide on the morning of her first GCSE exam. Both draw on real events.

What are we to make of this? Writers for teens have always kept a sharp eye on the preoccupations of the generation for which they are writing: sniffing out the zeitgeist and tapping into the reality is part of what makes fiction for this age group work best.

Sex was cheerfully outed long ago in titles such as Judy Blume's *Forever*. Drugs followed, with the publication of Melvin Burgess's excellent *Junk*. Adults were disapproving but teen readers were at ease: there wasn't much in either that they didn't already know, somewhat to the dismay of their parents.

But is suicide the same? While almost all teenagers will experience either sex or drugs or both – they are, after all, pretty universal rites of passage – only a handful will have to go through the harrowing experience of the death of a close friend.

Yet suicide in novels – as in life – is the ultimate expression of the despair from which most teenagers suffer at some time, and exploring the existential angst of the teenage years has always been the stuff of teen fiction. As the suicides mount in real life, so will they in fiction – whether we like it or not.

23 August 2013

⇨ The above information is reprinted with kind permission from *The Guardian*. Please visit www.guardian.co.uk for further information.

MoD confirms more British soldiers commit suicide than are killed in battle

Panorama *discover that at least 50 serving and veteran soldiers took their own lives in 2012.*

By Heather Saul

More British soldiers and veterans took their own lives last year than were killed in battle, it has emerged.

The Ministry of Defence confirmed that in 2012 seven serving soldiers were confirmed to have killed themselves, while a further 14 died in suspected suicides but inquests had yet to be held.

Although the Government does not record suicides among former soldiers, an investigation by the BBC's *Panorama* revealed that 21 serving soldiers and 29 veterans committed suicide in 2012.

The 50 suicides exceeds the 40 soldiers who died fighting the Taliban in Afghanistan during the same period.

Panorama obtained the total number of suicides by serving soldiers from a Freedom of Information request to the Ministry of Defence. They also contacted every coroner in the country to ask for the names of soldiers and veterans who killed themselves in 2012 and analysed newspaper reports of coroners' inquests.

Lance Sergeant Dan Collins who survived a bomb blast while serving

in Helmand Province in Afghanistan in 2009, killed himself on New Year's Eve in 2011 after suffering with Post Traumatic Stress Disorder, the BBC reported.

His mother Deana told *Panorama* her son was a 'victim of war' and his name should be added to the National Memorial Arboretum in Staffordshire which honours the military casualties of every conflict since WWII.

'Soldiers with PTSD are exactly the same. They're victims of war and they should be treated exactly the same,' she said.

A spokesman for the MoD said suicide among members of the Armed Forces remains 'extremely rare' and is lower than comparative rates in the civilian population.

An MoD spokesman said: 'Every suicide is a tragedy and our thoughts remain with the families of all those who have sadly taken their own lives.

'Mental health of our personnel and veterans is a top priority for the Government. That is why we have committed £7.4 million to ensure there is extensive mental health support in place for everyone who needs it.

'Medical experts and clinicians working in our Armed Forces and across the NHS are committed to providing the best possible care to all those that have bravely served their country and to ensuring a smooth transition from the Armed Forces into the NHS.'

Commodore Andrew Cameron, chief executive of Combat Stress, said: 'Every

suicide by a soldier or veteran is one too many but 50 in one year is desperately sad. Our thoughts go out to the families and friends affected. If confirmed, these figures remind us that serving in the armed forces can be very traumatic and can result in psychological as well as physical wounds.

'The priority now needs to be to ensure that the NHS must have a greater understanding of how to support soldiers and veterans suffering from service-related mental ill-health.

'The NHS and emergency services are generally the first organisations to have contact with a veteran in emotional turmoil. We are working with the NHS to increase awareness and improve responsiveness to veterans who need help and treatment when they are in crisis.

'Moreover, priority needs to be maintained on ensuring that serving personnel and veterans are educated about the signs of mental trauma and where to seek help. Identifying those in need and preventing suicides can be incredibly difficult. A greater focus should be placed on identifying soldiers and veterans suffering in silence with mental wounds so they can get the help and support required before it is too late.'

The *Panorama* special, *Broken By Battle*, will be broadcast on BBC One tomorrow at 9pm.

14 July 2013

⇨ The above information is reprinted with kind permission from *The Independent*. Please visit www.independent.co.uk for further information.

Train stations set for changes in drive to cut rail suicides

Measures being introduced or considered include extra fencing between platforms, 'trespass bollards' and closer monitoring.

By James Meikle

Train passengers are about to see the biggest changes in station design for years, and will have their behaviour monitored more closely, as part of a drive to cut suicides on the railways, which last year numbered 238.

Extra fencing, removal of seats from the ends of platforms, more no-go areas painted with yellow cross-hatching and 'trespass bollards' where the interruption of infrared beams sets off alarms will be among the most visible alterations.

Less obvious may be the use of smart cameras programmed to identify unusual behaviour, already being trialled at one busy station, and sensor lighting for dark areas. Network Rail is also considering whether tracking people's movements via mobile phone signals would help to alert control rooms to potential incidents.

Nearly 5,000 rail staff have been on courses developed by the Samaritans to help them identify and approach potentially suicidal people. The charity also provides trauma support for train and railway workers.

Who's that?

The other suicide victim... the train driver.

The introduction of fencing to separate platforms for fast through trains from those for stopping services has started, with stations between Reading and London Paddington and Milton Keynes and Euston the first affected.

Other moves designed to provide psychological disincentives are on the way, as are station watch schemes along on the lines of neighbourhood watch anti-crime groups.

Posters advertising the Samaritans and dedicated telephones at stations have already been introduced. The removal of 700 level crossings over the past three years has helped cut easy access to tracks. For the first time, railways are recording suicide attempts that staff action or other interventions have prevented. There are thought to have been at least 50 in the past year.

Network Rail says the partnership – also involving British Transport police, train operating companies, and rail safety advisers – has helped keep annual suicide numbers static at 238 in each of the past two years. Disruption to train services, which costs about £33 million a year according to Network Rail, has fallen by nearly a quarter in 12 months, and total delays due to suicide attempts have fallen from more than 6,500 hours to under 5,000.

Training police officers who respond to fatal incidents to undertake initial crime scene tasks has helped cut the time for dealing with unexplained deaths on the railways by a third, to 84 minutes, a process helped by dedicated phone lines from train cabs allowing drivers to give initial descriptions of incidents.

Neil Henry, Network Rail's head of performance and operations, said:

'From a purely economic point of view, there is a very strong business case which we don't deny. But there is certainly, too, a moral obligation, we feel, to do everything we can.'

Trials of new measures were encouraging, he said. 'You program cameras, for example, to focus on somebody who has been in the same location for a long time, has been on a station for a long time, perhaps has been there when a train has come in and not got on … It will then alert people that you have got somebody here that is acting out of the ordinary,' said Henry.

The fencing along the middle of platforms was 'not necessarily that difficult to get over but it is a barrier that may just change people's minds. There is evidence to suggest it does.'

Henry said although the partnerships with the Samaritans had been in place for nearly three years, an industry conference on the issue in June had proved a turning point. 'There was this noise going round that actually there is not much we can do, other than to restore the railways to normal working as quickly as possible. To prevent someone who is intent on taking their own life is too difficult. It was quite important to say some [suicide attempts] are preventable, we can really make a difference here.'

Railways in other countries, including Denmark, The Netherlands, Australia and Canada, are looking at the UK's progress. Rail suicides make up less than 4% of the UK total: there were 6,045 suicides in all in the UK in 2011, the highest total since 2004.

Police crime scene examiners normally attend unexplained or suspicious deaths, but 55 response officers in more remote areas have been equipped with forensic suits, cameras, swab kits and sterile evidence bags and have been trained to carry out body recovery and initial investigations. Coroners have been encouraged to standardise their procedures. 'We ensure the respect due to the deceased but minimise disruption to the wider railway network', said chief inspector Tom Naughton, the officer leading the strategy.

Initial interviews with drivers were not 'overly oppressive' or formal, he said, but together with other information gained from the scene, including an initial search of the body, could speed up investigations that were reviewed carefully later.

A pilot scheme in London is bringing in health professionals to police custody suites to assess those in mental distress, said Naughton. 'If someone is on the railway and they are obviously trespassing, putting themselves in danger, our priority is to get them into a place of safety. We don't want people criminalised if they are in need of medical aid.'

Rachel Kirby-Rider, executive director of fundraising and communications at Samaritans, called the developments 'an outstanding example of co-operation between industry and the charity sector'. The charity's research indicates that men in their 30–50s from disadvantaged backgrounds are at highest risk of dying by suicide, including on railways, and it is working with journalists to reduce 'copycat' suicides through more responsible reporting.

'We are doing everything we can to let people know that anyone can call Samaritans at any time,' she said. The Samaritans' 24-hour helpline is 08457 909090.

6 September 2013

⇨ The above information is reprinted with kind permission from *The Guardian*. Please visit www.guardian.co.uk for further information.

UK suicide rate amongst males reaches ten-year high in 2011 and overall number rises 'significantly'

The male suicide rate in Britain hit its highest level in nearly a decade in 2011 whilst the overall number of people taking their own life in Britain increased 'significantly'.

A total of 6,045 suicides were recorded among people aged 15 and over, the Office for National Statistics (ONS) said on Tuesday, up 437 or 8% on the previous year.

The number of male suicides increased 8% to 4,552, which at a rate of 18.2 per 100,000 was the highest level since 2002.

Female suicides also rose 8% to 1,493 or a rate of 5.6 per 100,000.

Two reports last year looked into the reasons behind suicides in the UK.

One, by sociologists from Cambridge University, attributed 1,000 suicides to 'economic recession, rising unemployment and biting austerity measures' from 2008–10.

Another by the Samaritans, explored the reasons for suicide beyond mental health problems among middle-aged men and found a loss of masculine pride and identity can tip them over the edge, leaving them more likely to commit suicide.

It found that on average about 3,000 middle-aged men from disadvantaged backgrounds take their own lives each year

Last year the Government announced a further £1.5 million in funding for research into suicide prevention among those most at risk of taking their own lives.

The pledge came as ministers unveiled a new suicide prevention strategy which aims to cut the suicide rate and provide more support to bereaved families.

The overall suicide rate in the UK increased from 11.1 to 11.8 per 100,000, the ONS said, while the highest suicide rate was among men aged 30 to 44 at 23.5 deaths per 100,000.

Among women, the highest rate of suicide was among 45- to 59-year-olds at 7.3 per 100,000.

In 2011, additional guidance was given to improve the classification of narrative verdicts at inquests in England and Wales.

A narrative verdict is a long-form, factual record of how and in what circumstances a death occurred and is used as an alternative to short-form verdicts such as suicide.

There had been concerns among researchers that these classification rules forced the ONS to record probable suicides as accidents.

So in 2011, the ONS identified common phrases used by coroners to terms allowed for the classification of intentional self-harm.

This additional guidance could have resulted in an increased number of narrative verdicts coded as intentional self-harm in 2011, the ONS said, which in turn could have contributed to the increase in the suicide rate.

If you are affected by any of the issues raised call The Samaritans on 08457 90 90 90.

22 January 2013

⇨ The above information is reprinted with kind permission from *The Huffington Post UK*. Please visit www. huffingtonpost.co.uk for further information.

Suicide: the 's' word

Suicide. There is something about that word that strikes fear in the strongest of people, stirs stigma in those that seem so savvy when it comes to mental health. I am sad to say, I am one of those people.

I find myself talking about mental health on a near daily basis. I write blogs, articles, speak to others, educate anyone and everyone that will listen about the trials and tribulations of living in the shadows of society when you have a mental health condition. In spite of this, I find myself rarely mentioning the 's' word. Despite having gone through an 's' situation myself.

Five years ago, I had a complete mental breakdown. I went from smiley and successful to housebound and horrified in the space of 24 hours. My life changed over night. I found myself on waiting lists, taking medication I didn't really understand, completely alone, with no-one to talk to and no-one who understood.

To this day, I stand by the idea that finding yourself with a mental health condition is a sure-fire way of weeding out the so-called associates that masquerade as 'mates' until you really need a shoulder to cry on.

I dropped to a level of depression that I barely knew existed. The world passed by without me in it, slipping away day by day, and I couldn't imagine me ever being a part of it again.

I took what I thought and felt at the time was a 'rational' decision. I cancelled meetings, social commitments, I said goodbye, I wrote letters. Fortunately one true friend at the time realised what was happening and ensured I was rushed to A&E to ensure my safety.

Even typing out the details, its hard for me to look back on. I feel ashamed, embarrassed. It feels like it happened to a whole other person. But it didn't. It happened to me. A depressed, in need of help and support with nowhere to turn or talk to, me.

It's always at this point I tell myself off. Talking about suicide shouldn't feel embarrassing. Nor should I be ashamed of something so serious. Something that is a 'something' that needs support and so much understanding. My views of 'reality' at the time were so messed up and misconstrued. I was ill. Very ill indeed. And that isn't my fault. It was something that needed treatment and counselling. But due to the stigma, I kept silent – rather

than speaking out for the support I so desperately needed.

I shouldn't be ashamed of something that affects so many. Suicide shouldn't be a dirty word, yet of all mental health 'words' it seems to be the dirtiest of all.

If by speaking out I can stop the stigma attached to suicide, then this is worth every difficult sentence and syllable.

World Suicide Prevention Day is about understanding, awareness, and most importantly, helping those hiding away in need of help they so thoroughly deserve. There is support out there and people who understand. There is a way out. There is a light at the end of the ever-darkening tunnel. It's knowing in which direction you need to look.

In those moments when you (or someone you love) feel so alone and afraid, with the grips of debilitating depression slowly squeezing the life from you – remember there are people out there that can hold your hand, people that can help, people that can tell you that yes – things will be OK. This doesn't have to be the end of your story.

Let us all speak out, and start being more honest with each other and most importantly – ourselves. Because by doing so – it's not just our own endings that we can re-write, but it will end the story of stigma attached to suicide – hopefully writing it out of the long-term picture altogether.

And that would be a very happy ending indeed.

10 September 2013

⇨ The above information is reprinted with kind permission from Mind. Please visit www.mind.org.uk for further information.

What Stephen Fry's conversation about suicide means to me

By Shea Wong

I'm sitting on a park bench. My makeup is sliding off the side of my face in the sun. I'm trying to look normal, whatever that is. I'm staring down the eyes of my interviewer, lest I let them wander over to the cameraman. I'm a little scared.

Yesterday, Stephen Fry revealed that in 2012 he had attempted suicide. As the President of Mind and the de facto face of the mental health anti-stigma initiative in the UK, his announcement was a sad but poignant reminder that bipolar, and indeed all mental illness, does not discriminate. A person who appears to have the world can suffer just as terribly as someone like me.

I got the call from Time to Change a few hours ago. They'd been understandably swamped with media requests to talk about Mr Fry, and could I spare an afternoon to chat? As a media volunteer this isn't a new thing for me, but I will admit when I hung up the phone, I was more nervous about an interview than I had ever been. I had never told anyone before, but I had suicide ideation early in my diagnosis.

There are over 500 books in my house. At least 40 of them are journals of mine, oversized beasts with papers stuck in them, and little pocket-sized notepads with scribbles, and fancy pants ones from the British Library, or moleskin covered. But there is one hidden away, that I've carried from home to home, and over the Atlantic, that is empty. That one was to be the final journal.

When I was initially diagnosed with bipolar, I saw it as a death sentence. It would be the thing that killed me. There was no point in attempting to have a 'normal' life, or to live for that matter. So, I bought a beautiful journal. And I would fill it with my writings, and drawings, and stuff. And when I was done, and that journal was filled to the brim with me, I would kill myself. Not the most reasonable course of self-treatment, but as Stephen Fry said, you can't reason your way out of depression, as it isn't reasonable. I took solace in knowing that once the journal was finished, at least I'd have something worthwhile to show for my life. I'd have created something of worth.

I never started that journal. The depression passed, and by the time the next cycle came, I had learned better coping skills. I eventually found love, and we began a family. But I never forgot what that journal stood for, and every day it is a reminder of how far I've come in spite of this illness.

I wish Stephen only the very best on his continued road through bipolar. If you feel as though you have no one to turn to, please contact the Samaritans and your local GP. I'm really glad that his producer found Mr Fry before it was too late. I'm really glad I never touched that journal again.

I'm really glad you are reading this. I'm really glad you are here.

6 June 2013

⇨ The above information is reprinted with kind permission from Time to Change. Please visit www.time-to-change.org.uk for further information.

Cyberbullying suicides: what will it take to have Ask.fm shut down?

As another teenage suicide is linked to the social-networking website, pressure grows on its foreign owners, parents and our Government to act.

By Joe Shute

When Charron Pugsley-Hill opened the newspaper on Tuesday morning, she was met by photographs of yet another smiling teenager staring up from the page.

Hannah Smith, 14, from Lutterworth, Leicestershire, was found hanged on Friday at the home she shared with her parents after receiving a series of abusive messages – which told her to 'drink bleach', 'go get cancer' and 'go die' – on the social-networking website Ask.fm. She is the latest British teenager to have taken her own life following severe bullying on the site.

Four deaths have been linked to it since September, when Pugsley-Hill's 15-year-old niece Ciara Pugsley was found dead in woodland near her home in County Leitrim, Ireland. Ciara had everything to live for. She loved riding her pony, represented her school at Gaelic football and came from a tight-knit family.

But she fell victim to bullies on the Latvia-based website, which allows its 65 million users to post questions and comments to each other, anonymously if they want, and has been described by child-safety experts as a 'stalker's paradise'. Her family had no idea of the horrific comments Ciara was being subjected to, until it was too late.

'She was a very feisty girl who was destined to make her mark on the world,' says Pugsley-Hill, a 48-year-old artist and designer who lives in Peterborough with her financial adviser husband, Tom, and their two young sons.

'She wasn't the sort of girl who would sit in the corner. That is why it was so shocking. For this to happen to her means it could happen to anybody.

'Every death since just hits me utterly. It's horrendous and completely brings it back. I now know there is another family having to go through what we are going through.'

Chances are that you may not even have heard of the social-networking website, which was founded in 2010 by Russian brothers and Internet entrepreneurs Ilya and Mark Terebin, the sons of a wealthy former Red Army serviceman. But Ask.fm gains 300,000 new and predominantly teenage users a day. Its iPhone app, launched in June, was last week reported to be among the most popular in the world.

Last month, a top grammar school became the first in Britain to ask parents to ban the site (and other social-networking pages) after an 'exponential increase' in pupils self-harming. *The Daily Telegraph* has also seen a warning letter sent in May from a Hampshire college to the parents of pupils, after two students reported having suffered abuse on the site.

Hannah's death has prompted her parents to join calls from others in Ireland, Britain, America, Australia and New Zealand for Ask.fm to be banned. But the site is based in Riga – the Terebin brothers are graduates of the Latvian capital's International School of Economics – and is governed by Latvian laws. It takes its domain name, .fm, from the Federated States

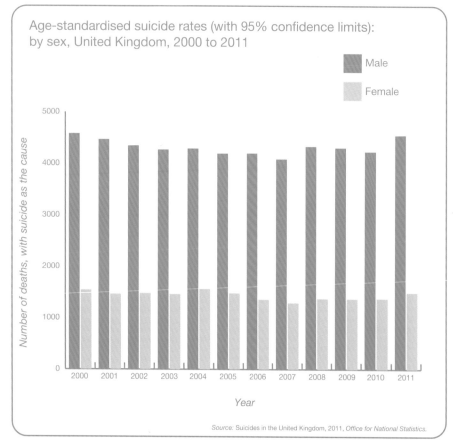

Age-standardised suicide rates (with 95% confidence limits): by sex, United Kingdom, 2000 to 2011

Male

Female

Number of deaths, with suicide as the cause

5000
4000
3000
2000
1000
0

2000 2001 2002 2003 2004 2005 2006 2007 2008 2009 2010 2011

Year

Source: Suicides in the United Kingdom, 2011, *Office for National Statistics.*

of Micronesia, a group of islands in the Pacific, as it is supposedly 'global and inclusive' in its appeal.

Last night, Ask.fm released a statement describing the latest death as a 'true tragedy' and said it would co-operate with the Leicestershire Police investigation. But in May, Mark Terebin, 28, claimed that in 90 per cent of cyber-bullying cases, teenagers actually posted the nasty comments themselves as a means to get attention. In a statement given to an Irish broadcaster, following the suicide of 13-year-old Erin Gallagher from County Donegal, last October, he appeared to suggest that British children were to blame for the recent tragedies.

'We have only this situation in Ireland and the UK most of all,' he said. 'It seems that children are more cruel in these countries.'

The Daily Telegraph asked a PR company hired by the firm to clarify these comments, as well as homophobic ones reportedly made by the brothers on their Ask.fm pages. No response has been received.

'I think there are many good things about social-networking sites,' says Pugsley-Hill. 'Occasionally I look on my 15-year-old's Facebook page and he's fine for me to do that. He is wedded to it. But if you say something face-to-face, you can see the effect it has. With cyber-bullying, you're in front of your computer, letting a stranger into your house.

'I don't think our politicians are doing enough, and I don't think we are taking the danger seriously enough. There are going to be a lot more [deaths] because of this.'

Campaigners claim that while online bullying is rife on other social-networking sites, Ask.fm is more worrying because it allows people to post comments in anonymity.

Messages found on Hannah's account in the past few weeks call her ugly and overweight. She was also bombarded by anonymous users urging her to commit suicide, including 'go die u pathetic emo' and 'do us all a favour n kill ur self'. Another wrote 'u ugly ---- go die evry1 wuld (sic) be happy.'

'These comments are extremely dangerous,' says Neil Roskilly, chief executive of the Independent Schools Association, which represents 325 schools. 'You will always get children who want to hide behind [their comments]. The anonymity allows them to do so.

'Sites like this are based overseas and our Internet service providers (such as Sky Broadband, Virgin Media and BT) don't seem to want to touch them at the moment. I find that very difficult. It's an area that the Government don't seem to want to touch either, despite the fact that the Prime Minister talks a lot about Internet pornography. He should be putting pressure on.'

The charity BeatBullying estimates one in three young people have been victims of cyber-bullying, with one in 13 experiencing persistent abuse. Of these, five per cent resorted to self-harm and three per cent reported an attempted suicide.

'There are children everywhere who are suffering in silence with depression and self-harming,' says Anthony Smythe, managing director of the charity. 'Bullying has moved from something that ends at the school gates to something always there – from the moment you wake up to the moment you go to bed.'

Ask.fm's terms of service say users must be 13 or older, although this can be ignored in a registration process that takes seconds. A statement from the website says it has 'policies in place that empower our users to protect themselves and to invite our intervention when required'. Users can switch off anonymous comments in their privacy settings, and if they do receive an offensive comment, they can block the user and report the incident. But campaigners say it needs better verification of users' details, better monitoring of abuse and clearer reporting procedures.

On the morning of Thursday, April 4, Joshua Unsworth, another young user of Ask.fm, should have been getting ready for a day at St Cecilia's High School in Longridge, near Preston. Instead, the 15-year-old victim of cyber-bullying was found hanging on land behind his home in the nearby village of Goosnargh. It has emerged that, a few months before he took his own life, he posted an anti-suicide video he'd made himself on YouTube.

'There was just to (sic) many suicides,' the Year 11 pupil wrote as an introduction to his video. 'I decided something needed to be done...'

Four months on from his death, it remains a chilling warning – frozen on our computer screens.

6 August 2013

⇨ The above information is reprinted with kind permission from *The Telegraph*. Please visit www.telegraph.co.uk for further information.

Consider a text for teen suicide prevention and intervention, research suggests

Adolescents commonly use social media to reach out when they are depressed.

Teens and young adults are making use of social networking sites and mobile technology to express suicidal thoughts and intentions as well as to reach out for help, two studies suggest.

An analysis of about one month of public posts on MySpace revealed 64 comments in which adolescents expressed a wish to die. Researchers conducted a follow-up survey of young adults and found that text messages were the second-most common way for respondents to seek help when they felt depressed. Talking to a friend or family member ranked first.

These young adults also said they would be least likely to use suicide hotlines or online suicide support groups – the most prevalent strategy among existing suicide-prevention initiatives.

The findings of the two studies suggest that suicide prevention and intervention efforts geared at teens and young adults should employ social networking and other types of technology, researchers say.

'Obviously this is a place where adolescents are expressing their feelings,' said Scottye Cash, associate professor of social work at The Ohio State University and lead author of the studies. 'It leads me to believe that we need to think about using social media as an intervention and as a way to connect with people.'

The research team is in the process conducting a study similar to the MySpace analysis by examining young people's Twitter messages for suicidal content. The researchers would like to analyse Facebook, but too few of the profiles are public, Cash said.

Suicide is the third leading cause of death among youths between the ages of ten and 24 years, according to the US Centers for Disease Control and Prevention (CDC).

Cash and colleagues published the MySpace research in a recent issue of the journal *Cyberpsychology, Behavior and Social Networking*. They presented the survey findings at a meeting of the American Academy of Child and Adolescent Psychiatry.

Cash's interest in this phenomenon was sparked in part by media reports about teenagers using social media to express suicidal thoughts and behaviours.

'We wanted to know: is that accurate, or are these isolated incidents? We found that in a short period of time, there were dozens of examples of teens with suicidal thoughts using MySpace to talk to their friends,' she said.

The researchers performed a content analysis of public profiles on MySpace. They downloaded profile pages of a 41,000-member sample of 13- to 24-year-olds from 3–4 March 2008, and again in December 2008, this time with comments included. By developing a list of phrases to identify potential suicidal thoughts or behaviours, the researchers narrowed two million downloaded comments to 1,083 that contained suggestions of suicidality, and used a manual process to eventually arrive at 64 posts that were clear discussions of suicide.

'There's a lot of drama and angst in teenagers so in a lot of cases, they might say something "will kill them" but not really mean it. Teasing out that hyperbole was an intense process,' Cash said. Song lyrics also made up a surprising number of references to suicide, she added.

The three most common phrases within the final sample were 'kill myself' (51.6 per cent), 'want to die' (15.6 per cent) and 'suicide' (14.1 per cent). Though in more than half of the posts the context was unknown, Cash and colleagues determined

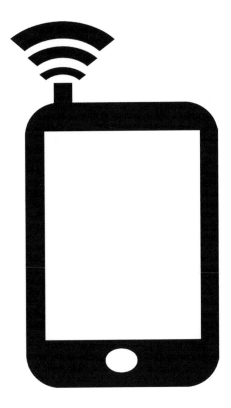

that 42 per cent of the posts referred to problems with family or other relationships – including 15.6 per cent that were about break-ups – and 6.3 per cent were attributable to mental health problems or substance abuse.

Very few of the posts identified the method the adolescents would consider in a suicide attempt, but three per cent mentioned guns, 1.6 per cent referred to a knife and 1.6 per cent combined being hit by a car and a knife.

With this information in hand, Cash and co-investigator Jeffrey Bridge of the Research Institute at Nationwide Children's Hospital surveyed young people to learn more about how they convey their depression and suicidal thoughts. Bridge also co-authored the MySpace paper.

Collaborating with Research Now, a social marketing firm, the researchers obtained a sample of survey participants through a company that collects consumer opinions. The final sample included 1,089 participants age 18–24 with an average age of almost 21, half male and half female, and 70.6 per cent white.

They were asked about their history of suicidal thoughts and attempts, general Internet and technology use, social networking activity and whether they had symptoms of depression.

More than a third reported they have had suicidal thoughts; of those, 37.5 per cent had attempted suicide, resulting in a 13 per cent rate of suicide attempts among the entire sample. That figure compares to the eight per cent of US high-school students who reported in a 2011 CDC national survey that they had attempted suicide at least once in the previous year. According to that survey, almost 16 per cent of youths had seriously considered suicide and almost 13 per cent had made a suicide plan in the previous 12 months.

'Obviously this is a place where adolescents are expressing their feelings. It leads me to believe that we need to think about using social media as an intervention and as a way to connect with people.'

Results of Cash's survey showed that respondents would favour talking to a friend or family member when they were depressed, followed by sending texts, talking on the phone, using instant messaging and posting to a social networking site. Less common responses included talking to a health-care provider, posting to a blog, calling a suicide prevention hotline and posting to an online suicide support group.

Response trends suggested, though, that participants with suicidal thoughts or attempts were more willing to use technology – specifically the phone, instant messaging, texting and social networking – to reach out compared to those with no suicidal history. In light of this trend, the fact that the participants were active online consumers might have contributed to the relatively high percentage of suicide attempts among the study sample. In addition, the survey also asked about lifetime suicide history, not just recent history, Cash noted.

The survey also showed that this age group looks to the Internet for information on sensitive topics, and again suggested that young adults of both sexes with a history of suicidal thoughts or attempts consulted the Internet for information about topics that are difficult to discuss – specifically drug use, sex, depression, eating disorders or other mental health concerns. Females with past suicide attempts used social networking the most, according to the results.

'It appears that our methods of reaching out to adolescents and young adults is not actually meeting them where they are. If, as adults, we're saying, 'this is what we think you need' and they tell us they're not going to use it, should we keep pumping resources into suicide hotlines?' Cash said. 'We need to find new ways to connect with them and help them with whatever they're struggling with, or, in other words, meet them where they are in ways that make sense to them.'

A notable resource already available is www.reachout.com, a website geared toward adolescents who are struggling through a tough time. Some Internet-based resources exist that could serve as models for new suicide prevention interventions, she noted. They include teen.smokefree.gov and www.thatsnotcool.com.

The survey research was supported by an Ohio State University College of Social Work Seed Grant.

Additional co-authors of the MySpace paper include Michael Thelwall of the University of Wolverhampton in the United Kingdom, Sydney Peck of Elmira College and Jared Ferrell of the University of Akron.

24 June 2013

⇨ The above information is reprinted with kind permission from Ohio State University. Please visit www.researchnews.osu.edu for further information.

Key facts

- About one in three people who self-harm for the first time will do it again during the following year. (page 3)

- About one in 100 people who self-harm over 15 years will actually kill themselves. This is more than 50 times the rate for people who don't self-harm. The risk increases with age and is much greater for men. (page 3)

- 33% of people believe that finding support is nearly always a reason a young person stops self-harming. Only 9% believe that the reason young people stop self-harming is because they 'grow out of it'. (page 4)

- 16% of parents, teachers and GPs believe that young people can easily stop harming if they want to. (page 5)

- 34% of parents, teachers and GPs believe that young people self-harm because it is 'fashionable'. (page 5)

- 29% of young people say that TV or radio has influenced their view of self-harm. (page 6)

- 11% of young people say that talking to mental health professionals has shaped their view of self-harm and 19% say that talking to a teacher has shaped their views. (page 6)

- A recent report found that 43% of young people know someone who has self-harmed, but one-in-four didn't know what to say to a friend who was self-harming. (page 8)

- One in 12 children and young people are said to self-harm. (page 10)

- Over the last ten years inpatient admissions for young people who self-harm have increased by 68%. (page 10)

- One in five children have symptoms of depression, and almost a third have thought about or attempted suicide before they were 16. (page 16)

- A recent survey by YouGov found that nearly a third of young people have self-harmed because they feel 'down' and over half of those who had shown signs of depression felt let down by their experiences of mental health support. (page 16)

- Almost one in five young people say they have felt constantly on edge in the last two weeks, a YouGov survey says. (page 16)

- A study has found that children are most likely to speak to their friends about mental health issues (57%), followed by parents (54%) and a face-to-face counsellor (32%). (page 16)

- Around 4,400 people end their own lives in England each year. (page 20)

- Around 75% of suicides are men and in almost all cultures, the suicide rates rise with age. (page 20)

- The highest suicide rates in the UK are among people aged 75 or over. (page 20)

- Around 90% of suicide victims suffer from a psychiatric disorder at the time of their death. (page 20)

- Over 1,000 men aged 50+ end their own lives every year in England and Wales. (page 20)

- Among young people, 80% of suicides are male. (page 20)

- There were 1,333 suicides among mental health patients in England in 2011. (page 21)

- One in ten children of school age suffers from a diagnosable mental health disorder. (page 28)

- In 2012 there were 238 suicides on the railways in the UK. (page 32)

- In 2011, the male suicide rate in Britain reached its highest level in nearly a decade. (page 33)

Bipolar disorder

Previously called manic depression, this illness is characterised by mood swings where periods of severe depression are balanced by periods of excitement and overactivity (mania).

Cognitive behavioural therapy (CBT)

A psychological treatment which assumes that behavioural and emotional reactions are learned over a long period. A cognitive therapist will seek to identify the source of emotional problems and develop techniques to overcome them.

Copycat suicides

In rare cases, an individual may choose to take their own life because they have heard about others doing so, or have been exposed to suicide via the media. Or they may choose to commit suicide using a particular method they have become aware of due to media exposure. A famous recent example is the spate of copycat suicides which took place in Bridgend, Wales, in 2008, when a total of approximately 24 teenagers took their lives, the majority of whom did not know each other. Internet suicide 'cults' or 'pacts' have also been blamed for serial suicides.

Depression

Someone is said to be significantly depressed, or suffering from depression, when feelings of sadness or misery don't go away quickly and are so bad that they interfere with everyday life. Symptoms can also include low self-esteem and a lack of motivation.

Group therapy

These are meetings for people who are seeking help for a problem (in this case, self-harm or suicidal thoughts) and are led by trained specialists. They differ from self-help groups in that an expert is present to run the meeting and provide professional advice and support.

Overdosing

Overdosing involves taking a larger quantity of a particular drug or medication than is safe, sometimes inadvertently but often as an act of self-harm (this may be referred to as self-poisoning) or as an attempt to kill oneself. Although overdoses don't always lead to death, sometimes the drugs ingested can cause irreversible damage to the liver and other vital organs.

Self-harm/self-injury

Self-harm is the act of deliberately injuring or mutilating oneself. People injure themselves in many different ways, including cutting, burning, poisoning or hitting parts of their body. Self-harmers often see harming as a coping strategy and give a variety of motivations for hurting themselves, including relieving stress or anxiety, focusing emotional pain and as a way of feeling in control. Although prevalent in young people, self-harm is found amongst patients of all ages. It is not usually an attempt to commit suicide, although people who self-harm are statistically more likely to take their own lives than those who don't.

Suicide

Suicide is the act of taking one's own life. Men are statistically more likely to take their own life than women, and suffering from a mental illness such as depression, bipolar disorder or schizophrenia is also a risk factor for suicide. Elderly people are also considered vulnerable as they are more likely to have to deal with traumatic life events such as bereavement and ill health.

Talking therapies

These involve talking and listening. Some therapists will aim to find the root cause of a sufferer's problem and help them deal with it, some will help to change behaviour and negative thoughts, while others simply offer support.

Assignments

Brainstorming

⇨ In small groups, or as a class, discuss the issues surrounding self-harm. Consider the following questions:

- Why do some people self-harm?

- What help is available for people who self-harm?

- Is self-harm an easy topic to discuss? Who would you be most likely to discuss it with?

- How do you think the media portrays people who self-harm?

⇨ In small groups, or as a class, discuss the issues surrounding suicide. Consider the following questions:

- Are suicide and self-harm related?

- What should someone do if they start to experience suicidal thoughts?

- Is suicide a topic that is talked about in schools? Do you think it should be?

Research

⇨ A recent report from the Samaritans found that male suicide rates have increased. Go to their website and find the report *Men and Suicide, why it's a social issue*. Read the executive summary and then choose one section (personality traits, masculinity, etc.) and read it in full. Create a bullet point list of the things in your chosen section that contribute to male suicide rates and then feedback to your class.

⇨ Research mental health services in your local area and find out where you could go for help if you had suicidal thoughts or were self-harming.

Design

⇨ Design an information booklet that could be distributed throughout your school, or college, to raise awareness of the issues surrounding self-harm. Use the articles in Chapter 1 to help you, and refer to the guide on *Reporting suicide and self-harm* on page 1 for guidelines on how you should display and present your material.

⇨ Design a poster that will encourage people who may be experiencing suicidal feelings to seek help. Make sure you refer to the *Reporting suicide and self-harm* guide on page 1, and carefully consider how you can promote the issue without sensationalising it.

⇨ Design an app that could help people who self-harm.

Oral

⇨ With a partner, discuss the steps you could take if a friend confided in you that he/she was experiencing suicidal thoughts.

⇨ In pairs or small groups, choose one of the illustrations from this book and discuss what you think the artist was trying to portray with this image. Do you think it is successful?

⇨ Read the article *What I'm thinking about... teen suicides in fiction* on page 30. In pairs or small groups, discuss whether you believe that suicide is a topic which should be tackled in young adult fiction.

⇨ Why might the recession be a possible factor in the increase in suicide rates? Discuss as a group.

Reading/writing

⇨ Imagine that you are a campaigner who is working to have Ask.fm shut down because of its recent links to teen suicides. Write a blog post explaining your point of view and giving reasons why you believe the site shouldn't continue to run.

⇨ Read the article *Consider a text for teen suicide prevention and intervention...* on page 38. Write a summary of the article for your school newspaper.

⇨ Write a guide for parents, giving advice about what they can do if they have a son/daughter who self-harms.

⇨ Write a two-page essay that explores the question, 'Are self-harm and suicide related?'

⇨ Read the article *'Controlled self-harm' policy leaves school under investigation* on page 19. Write a letter to *The Guardian* newspaper, explaining whether you agree or disagree with the school's decision.

⇨ Visit Stephen Fry's website and research his work with the mental health charity Mind. Do you think it is a good thing for celebrities such as Stephen Fry to speak out about mental illness and suicide? Write a one-page essay or a blog post exploring this question.

Index

Acknowledgements

The publisher is grateful for permission to reproduce the material in this book. While every care has been taken to trace and acknowledge copyright, the publisher tenders its apology for any accidental infringement or where copyright has proved untraceable. The publisher would be pleased to come to a suitable arrangement in any such case with the rightful owner.

Images

Cover, page iii and page 19: MorgueFile, page 1: iStock, page 8: iStock, page 15: iStock, page 21: MorgueFile, page 30: iStock, page 31 © Ministry of Defence, page 34: MorgueFile, page 35: iStock, page 37: iStock.

Illustrations

Page 2: Simon Kneebone, page 14: Don Hatcher, page 17: Angelo Madrid, page 25: Don Hatcher, page 32: Angelo Madrid, page 38: Simon Kneebone.

Additional acknowledgements

Editorial on behalf of Independence Educational Publishers by Cara Acred.

With thanks to the Independence team: Mary Chapman, Sandra Dennis, Christina Hughes, Jackie Staines and Jan Sunderland.

Cara Acred

Cambridge

January 2014